Kinda
VEGAN

Kinda VEGAN

200 Easy and Delicious Recipes for Meatless Meals
(When You Want Them)

Adams Media

New York   London   Toronto   Sydney   New Delhi

Aadamsmedia

Adams Media
An Imprint of Simon & Schuster, Inc.
57 Littlefield Street
Avon, Massachusetts 02322

First Adams Media hardcover edition January 2019

ADAMS MEDIA and colophon are trademarks of Simon & Schuster.

For information about special discounts for bulk purchases, please contact Simon & Schuster Special Sales at 1-866-506-1949 or business@simonandschuster.com.

The Simon & Schuster Speakers Bureau can bring authors to your live event. For more information or to book an event contact the Simon & Schuster Speakers Bureau at 1-866-248-3049 or visit our website at www.simonspeakers.com.

Interior design by Katrina Machado
Photographs by James Stefiuk

Manufactured in the United States of America

10 9 8 7 6 5 4 3 2 1

Library of Congress Cataloging-in-Publication Data
Title: Kinda vegan
Description: Avon, Massachusetts: Adams Media, 2019.
Includes index.
Identifiers: LCCN 2018037202 | ISBN 9781721400010 (hc) | ISBN 9781721400027 (ebook)
Subjects: LCSH: Vegan cooking. | Cookbooks.
Classification: LCC TX837 .K495 2019 | DDC 641.5/6362--dc23
LC record available at https://lccn.loc.gov/2018037202

ISBN 978-1-72140-001-0
ISBN 978-1-72140-002-7 (ebook)

Contains material adapted from the following titles published by Adams Media, an Imprint of Simon & Schuster, Inc.: *The Part-Time Vegan* by Cherise Grifoni, copyright © 2011, ISBN 978-1-4405-1226-1; *The Everything*® *Vegan Cookbook* by Jolinda Hackett with Lorena Novak Bull, copyright © 2010, ISBN 978-1-4405-0216-3.

The various uses of veganism as a health aid are based on tradition, scientific theories, or limited research. They often have not been thoroughly tested in humans, and safety and effectiveness have not yet been proven in clinical trials. Some of the conditions for which veganism can be used as a treatment or remedy are potentially serious, and should be evaluated by a qualified healthcare provider.

CONTENTS

CHAPTER 4: SALADS AND SALAD DRESSINGS.....67

CHAPTER 5: SOUPS.....93

CONTENTS

CHAPTER 6: EASY SIDES.....113

CHAPTER 7: CLASSIC MAIN DISHES: VEGAN TWISTS ON FAMILIAR FAVORITES.....143

CHAPTER 8: INTERNATIONAL MAIN DISHES.....179

CONTENTS

CHAPTER 9: SINFUL DESSERTS.....237

INTRODUCTION

Here's the deal: maybe you're looking to incorporate more plant-based meals into your diet but don't want to lose that "fried chicken Fridays" tradition. Or maybe you want to dip your toes into veganism first, getting your feet wet before deciding to make the change to a completely vegan lifestyle. That's where *Kinda Vegan* comes in: your no-nonsense guide to being vegan-*ish*. Restrictive dieting be gone; with *Kinda Vegan* you can go meatless on Monday, then enjoy a juicy steak dinner on Tuesday—no judgment.

Where do vegans get their protein? What can you possibly eat that doesn't have milk in it? Won't it taste horrible? Don't vegans eat only spinach and weeds? Well, kids, here's some news for you: you *can* have your cake and eat it too. And your ice cream. And your cheesy flavor. All you need are some conscious shopper skills and quick, go-to information. The first chapter of *Kinda Vegan* covers the basics of veganism, including the essential foods to have in your pantry. From grains and lentils to maple syrup and dairy-free milk alternatives, there are *tons* of delicious vegan ingredients to enjoy. No weeds here! Plus, you know that eating vegan saves our animal friends, but the other benefits of cutting down on those fatty meats and processed foods may surprise you. From weight loss and lowered blood sugar levels to a decreased risk of heart disease and certain cancers, you will be feeling fabulous—no need to thank us (though you can if you want to).

In *Kinda Vegan* you'll also discover 200 recipes, organized by meal, that are so tasty you won't believe they're vegan. It's easy to make a vegan meal—or day of meals—whenever you want. Plus, each recipe has a special icon to let you know whether the recipe is high in protein, is high in fiber, is especially quick to make, or can be adapted to substitute non-vegan ingredients. Hearty breakfast dishes like Crepes for

When You're Feeling Lazy and Whole-Wheat Brilliant Blueberry Muffins, international bites like Easy Falafel Patties and Chinese Fried Rice with Tofu and Cashews, and guilt-free desserts like Chocolate Mocha Ice Cream and Perfect Pumpkin Bread may just have you wanting to go vegan all week! Not the best at planning meals? Don't sweat it: we've also included an appendix of vegan meal plans. You can plan out a few days of meals in minutes, or you can flip to a meal plan whenever you are out of ideas or just don't have the energy to decide on what to eat that day. So whatever your reasons are for ditching meat, and whatever your schedule and taste buds desire, with *Kinda Vegan*, being veganish is a snap!

BEING VEGANISH

WHAT IS VEGANISM?

Veganism is the exclusion of all animal and animal-based products from your diet. This includes meat, eggs, dairy, and gelatin, and it can even extend to some types of sugar and honey. Fear not, faithful readers. There is always a delicious vegan way around these things. Perhaps you're finding yourself in a small predicament: you wish to be (kinda) vegan, but you have nowhere to turn. Maybe you have questions like these:

1. How do you start?
2. What ingredients do you start looking for?
3. And how the hell do you find them?

No worries. You don't need to take a transcontinental ship in order to scout out the new ingredients that will make your transition to veganism both easy and fun. That's what we are here for! Now granted, occasionally some vegans get a little weird. There are some recipes out there that include Irish moss, seaweed, algae, and even brains. Just kidding about the last part, but we're still talking about some unorthodox choices. Thankfully all of the recipes in this book will make use of your classic favorite ingredients, some soon-to-be new friends, and fresh produce.

HOW DO YOU START?

Some people can stop eating meat and animal by-products cold turkey. Maybe they were never really that into meat or dairy in the first place, or maybe they are just that disciplined. Others find it a huge struggle to be 100 percent vegan because of their love of poultry, beef, milk, cheese, or all of the above. Lesson: everyone's journey is different! Don't be ashamed of not following a specific dietary lifestyle 100 percent. It's always going to be a bit of an exploratory venture to find what works for you. Don't be discouraged if you have cravings for your meaty bygone loves. There is nothing wrong with those urges. You should listen to what your body has to say at all times, even if that means reevaluating your current choices.

ALLOW VEGANISM TO BE A HEALTHY ADDITION TO YOUR DIET

The lifestyle of veganism should be one you adapt to and adopt voluntarily. You don't have to go all-out vegan if you don't want to. Reserve cheese or milk for special occasions, certain days of the week, or holiday treats. Try going vegan for a month to increase your energy. Or do it once a year during the summer, when eating fresh and light makes you feel great. Be vegan when you want to be.

Our cavemen ancestors ate mostly meat and little else. They didn't drink cow's milk, and they certainly didn't eat cheese. They had no processed sugar or grains. Nowadays there is research to suggest that diets heavy in red or processed meat can lead to heart disease and other health problems. Moderation is the key for most diets, but in a lot of ways a go at veganism is giving your body the chance to thrive off what is naturally available from the earth around us.

VEGANISM AND HEALTH

Eating vegan is not a fad "diet" and should never be treated as one. It is a regimen that must be carefully monitored if adhered to tightly. Just like any other diet, veganism has its challenges. If vegans aren't careful, they will often miss out on vital nutrients such as B_{12}, B_6, calcium, iron, folic acid, and protein. Deficiencies can lead to anemia, fatigue, and other health problems. Thus, it is always important to talk with your healthcare provider before changing your eating patterns.

Enough with that serious stuff, though! If you eat vegan or kinda vegan, and if you keep a careful eye on what you consume (as with any other diet), you will be healthy, energetic, and feeling spectacular. The whole foods and fresh produce you will consume as a vegan will work toward a better, healthier you.

WHAT'S IN A VEGAN PANTRY, ANYWAY?

There is a whole *world* of ingredients you can use specifically in vegan cooking. Arrowroot, egg replacer, nut milks, and soy yogurt are just a few. But there are also old-time favorites that you will use again and again! Here is a helpful list of some vegan items you might find valuable to have in your cabinets:

- **AGAVE NECTAR:** A sweet syrup made from the agave plant of Mexico (the same plant used to make tequila). This is a vegan sweetener that people use in place of traditional sugar. Traditional sugar is often bleached with the use of animal bones. If you wish to be vegan about your traditional sugar (brown or white), just contact the manufacturer and ask if it bleaches!

- **COCONUT OIL:** Coconut oil can be heated to very high temperatures without changing its molecular form, which makes it perfect for stir-frying. Since it is solid at room temperature, it is also used widely in vegan baking to "set" vegan desserts like "cheese" cakes. To bake with coconut oil, usually you must melt the solid oil into its liquid form by submerging the oil container in hot water for one minute. You can also melt coconut oil for thirty seconds in the microwave.

- **EGG REPLACER:** There are many kinds of "egg replacers" on the market. Some are specifically sold as mixes in the natural foods section under the name of "egg replacer mix." Most of the time eggs are used as a binder in recipes, or they are added to keep the batter moist. Often the need for moisture can be easily taken care of by using bananas, applesauce, jam, or soy yogurt. Remember that these items add sugar content to the recipe, and you may wish to adjust recipe sweetness accordingly by adding a little less sweetener (sugar, honey, agave) than the recipe calls for.

THE SKINNY ON...HONEY

Honey is the subject of much debate in vegan circles because insects are killed during the harvesting of honey. Many vegans consider this a violation of their principles. Others note that bugs are killed in the harvesting of most fruits and vegetables. It's your call as to whether you want to eat honey.

- **GRAINS:** Grains include barley, millet, bulgur wheat, brown rice, and buckwheat. Use these when you tire of standard white rice. They have both fiber and protein.

- **LEGUMES:** Beans, lentils, and sprouted beans are all types of legumes. Also included in this category are black beans, chickpeas, kidney beans, black-eyed peas, cannellini beans, and lima beans. Legumes pack a powerful punch of vegan protein.

- **MAPLE SYRUP AND HONEY:** Here are two other nontraditional natural sweeteners that can take the place of sugar in almost any recipe. Remember that when you're baking with syrup and honey, your batter may become runnier because they are liquid. Add a little more flour to account for this.

- **NONDAIRY MILKS:** Soy, rice, almond, hazelnut, coconut, and even hemp milk are all tasty and creamy alternatives to traditional dairy milk. More and more varieties crop up in the supermarket every day. You can even find chocolate, vanilla, chai, and traditional holiday favorites like "eggnog" and autumn spice!

- **NUTRITIONAL YEAST:** Despite having the worst food name on the planet, this ingredient is a great source of vitamin B_{12} and protein. It's very inexpensive and lends a sharp "cheesy" flavor to many dishes. Nutritional yeast can also be sprinkled on toast, lettuce, or popcorn.

- **NUTS:** Cashews, pistachios, Brazil nuts, macadamias, walnuts, almonds, pecans—you name it! Nuts are great sources of protein and good-for-you fats.

- **PRODUCE:** Meet your new best friend. Go acquaint yourself with the produce section of your grocery store. You will be spending a lot of time there. Try to appreciate the fresh flavors of seasonal fruits and veggies, and pick foods for their ripeness and color. Slowly you will get to know the difference between an acorn squash and a butternut squash, or apricots and peaches! You can use veggies for so many things other than boring old salads—shaved spiced carrots are great substitutes for taco "meat," for example. (Trust us, it's good.)

- **QUINOA:** A South American grain eaten by the ancient Aztecs, quinoa is a powerhouse of proteins and vital nutrients. Quinoa makes a great alternative to rice and can be eaten hot or cold, sweet or savory.

- **SOY CREAM:** Coffee lovers everywhere will embrace soy cream. It's also great in many creamy rice or pasta dishes.

- **SPICES:** They say variety is the spice of life, but really spices are the spice of life. You can jazz up (or disguise, if that's how you roll) any vegetable on the planet with the flavors of garlic, turmeric, cumin, white and red pepper, basil, parsley, rosemary, cardamom, chicory, chili pepper, coriander, curry powder, ginger, thyme, sage, and tamarind.

- **TEMPEH, SEITAN, AND TVP:** These are terrific substitutes for meat proteins. Tempeh is made from fermented soybeans and has a chewy, crunchy texture that is an excellent addition to salads. Seitan is made from wheat gluten and usually comes in extremely thin slices. It is famous in the vegan world for its meat-like appearance, and like tempeh, it is flavorless and easily absorbs the flavor of any dish. TVP stands for "textured vegetable protein." Really, who is coming up with these horrible names? Anyway, TVP is also usually made from soy and can be found in most of your standard veggie burgers. All three substitutes can have a distinctly "meaty" texture if prepared properly!

- **TOFU:** Tofu, made from fermented soybeans, is a great protein-filled addition to stir-fries or salads. Tofu can be used in place of eggs in "scrambled eggs" or frittatas. You can also use it to make shakes, smoothies, quiches, pies, and love. (Well, maybe not love—unless you're counting how much you're going to enjoy the food.)

- **UNSWEETENED/BAKING CHOCOLATE, CAROB CHIPS, AND CACAO NIBS:** Who said vegans can't eat chocolate? Many vegan recipes include baking chocolate (which is pure chocolate with no added ingredients). Using baking chocolate shavings in a recipe that includes a sweetener like honey or maple syrup gives you chocolatey flavor and preserves the sweetness. Carob chips from the carob plant are nuttier and softer than chocolate, but they are just as good for cookies. Cacao is another plant with a nutty chocolate taste that adds a great crunch to things like banana bread.

- **VEGAN MARGARINE:** Most regular margarines also happen to be vegan. You can always check the label to be sure. However, many brands are processed on equipment that handles milk and thus may be "tainted." Simply look for one labeled vegan if this concerns you. Many brands of margarine marketed as vegan are also available soy-free.

AND WHERE DO YOU FIND THIS STUFF?

Cacao nibs? Seriously? Yes, seriously. It may seem like these things are a little bizarre, but most of the ingredients listed here should be sold at your local grocery store. Natural food chains like Whole Foods carry a few of the more "obscure" items like carob chips and soy yogurt. In the vegan world foods that are not marketed to vegan buyers yet still remain free of non-vegan ingredients are referred to as "accidentally vegan." Many foods that you would never expect to be vegan just happen to be. Oreos, for one. Many packaged brownie mixes, before you are instructed to add the egg, are also vegan. And now you know how to replace those pesky eggs. Savvy. On to the cooking!

CHAPTER 2

EASY BREAKFASTS

FOR PEOPLE WHO ARE ON THE GO, AND MORE TIME-CONSUMING BREAKFASTS FOR THOSE OF US WHO ARE LAZY AND HAVE LOTS OF TIME FOR EATING

CREPES FOR WHEN YOU'RE FEELING LAZY

Crepes have to be the absolute simplest thing to make. Once you've mastered the art of the flip, this will be your go-to recipe of the month. This recipe uses a heavenly blend of Purely Vegan Chocolate Hazelnut Spread and strawberries as its filling, but you can also fill the crepes with other sweet fruits, peanut butter, or savory onions, tomatoes, and garlic. Either way they're a great light meal you can assemble with anything you have on hand.

SERVES 4

1 cup whole-wheat flour

¾ cup plain unsweetened almond milk

½ cup water

2 teaspoons granulated sugar

1 teaspoon vanilla extract

¼ cup vegan margarine, melted

¼ teaspoon salt

1 cup Purely Vegan Chocolate Hazelnut Spread (see recipe in Chapter 3)

2 cups hulled, sliced fresh strawberries

1. Whisk all ingredients except Purely Vegan Chocolate Hazelnut Spread and strawberries together in a large bowl, and refrigerate for an hour. Remove and mix again.

2. Heat a large skillet over medium heat for approximately 1 minute before starting to cook. Lightly grease the skillet with vegan margarine. Swirl approximately ¼ cup of batter into the pan so that all edges are covered. Turn heat to medium-high and cook for 1 minute. Use a spatula to flip. Cook the other side for 1 minute. Crepes will be finished when very lightly browned. Repeat with remaining batter.

3. Spread each crepe with Purely Vegan Chocolate Hazelnut Spread, top with strawberries, and fold it up! Serve immediately.

Per Serving:
Calories: 420
Fat: 26 g
Protein: 8 g

Sodium: 314 mg
Fiber: 7 g
Carbohydrates: 42 g
Sugar: 15 g

EASY VEGAN BREAKFAST PARFAIT

Vegans can *so* eat yogurt. But you'll be searching for those made from soy, not cow's or goat's milk. There are so many variations of soy yogurt these days—and so many flavors—that you won't be hard-pressed to find a new favorite.

SERVES 2

1/4 cup flax meal

2 (6-ounce) containers vanilla soy yogurt

2 tablespoons maple syrup

1/2 cup granola

1/2 cup peeled, sliced fresh bananas

1. Mix flax, soy yogurt, and syrup together in a medium bowl.
2. Layer ingredients in two medium containers in this order: yogurt mixture, granola, bananas. Repeat until everything is used up.

Per Serving:
Calories: 444
Fat: 14 g
Protein: 13 g

Sodium: 36 mg
Fiber: 9 g
Carbohydrates: 68 g
Sugar: 41 g

HOMEMADE ALMOND MILK

The almond milk, soy milk, or rice milk that you purchase at the supermarket is usually loaded with sugar. Fruit and cereal contain enough sugar already, so why add more to your smoothies or breakfasts? Plus, homemade is the freshest you can get—sort of like milking your own cow. But without the cow. Or the milk. Or the hay. Or the fertilizer on your shoes.

YIELDS 1 QUART

1 cup raw almonds, soaked overnight and drained

4 cups water

1/2 teaspoon vanilla extract

1 tablespoon maple syrup

1/8 teaspoon salt

1. Process almonds and water in a blender until there are no lumps left.
2. Strain the purée through cheesecloth in order to catch any remaining pieces.
3. Stir in vanilla, syrup, and salt. Store covered in the refrigerator for up to 1 week.

Per Serving:
Calories: 222
Fat: 18 g
Protein: 8 g

Sodium: 74 mg
Fiber: 4 g
Carbohydrates: 11 g
Sugar: 5 g

BLACK QUINOA
BREAKFAST CEREAL

Do you gag at the thought of boring oatmeal? Crash after a sugar-laden breakfast cereal and are nearly comatose by the time 11:00 a.m. rolls around? This Black Quinoa Breakfast Cereal is a perfect way to start your day. Packed full of protein, antioxidants, and essential vitamins, it'll keep you running straight past the afternoon slump. If you don't have quinoa on hand, use brown rice. It's just as good!

SERVES 4

1 cup black quinoa

1½ cups water

1½ cups hulled, sliced fresh strawberries

½ cup peeled, sliced fresh bananas

½ cup fresh wolfberries (goji berries)

¾ cup raw cashews

2 tablespoons maple syrup

½ cup plain unsweetened almond milk

1. In a large saucepan, combine quinoa with water. Bring to a boil over high heat and then reduce to a simmer on low heat. Let simmer until all water is evaporated, approximately 20 minutes. Quinoa should be completely cooked. It's okay if it's a little crunchy!

2. Drain quinoa. Add fruit, cashews, and syrup. Top with milk.

Per Serving:
Calories: 291
Fat: 8 g
Protein: 9 g

Sodium: 29 mg
Fiber: 6 g
Carbohydrates: 48 g
Sugar: 14 g

CAROB PEANUT BUTTER SMOOTHIE

Dear reader: For those who constantly crave the creamy, nutty goodness of peanut butter and the subtle, hearty flavor of carob, and for those who wish to have an energizing, protein-filled smoothie to replace those bottled post-workout protein drinks, we cut down on the sugar and gave you some potassium. And you didn't even have to ask. Love, Peanut Butter

SERVES 2

8 ice cubes

2 medium bananas, peeled

2 tablespoons all-natural peanut butter

2 tablespoons carob powder

1 cup plain unsweetened almond milk

½ teaspoon apple juice

Blend all ingredients in a blender or food processor until smooth. Serve immediately.

Per Serving:
Calories: 234
Fat: 10 g
Protein: 6 g

Sodium: 99 mg
Fiber: 7 g
Carbohydrates: 37 g
Sugar: 19 g

TOP OF THE MORNING CASHEW BUTTER WRAP

Soft, filling, and sweet but not overly saccharine—this breakfast wrap will have everyone around you as green as the hills of Ireland. It's perfect if you stumbled out of bed after hitting snooze too many times and have to make a mad dash for your car. After all, you don't want to be late on an empty stomach, do you? You can also mix and match ingredients at your will!

YIELDS 1 WRAP

2 tablespoons cashew butter

1 (8") whole-wheat flour tortilla

2 tablespoons Kashi Honey Sunshine cereal

1/3 cup fresh blackberries

1 1/2 medium bananas, peeled and sliced thin

1/4 teaspoon ground allspice

1 tablespoon raisins

1/2 tablespoon maple syrup

1. Spread cashew butter onto tortilla. Layer with cereal, blackberries, and banana slices.
2. Add allspice and raisins, and drizzle with syrup. Fold or roll up the wrap tightly.
3. Warm in the microwave for about 12 seconds on high heat with the seam of the wrap facing down.

PART-TIME TIP
Fiber helps prevent the absorption of fat.

Per Serving:
Calories: 575
Fat: 22 g
Protein: 11 g

Sodium: 332 mg
Fiber: 13 g
Carbohydrates: 93 g
Sugar: 41 g

PEACH THYME MUFFINS

Talk about your potentially random combinations, right? The sharp tartness of peach and smooth, leafy taste of thyme really do make the perfect combination. These muffins are delightfully aromatic and pair perfectly with a glass of orange juice and a drizzle of honey.

YIELDS 18 MUFFINS

2 cups whole-wheat flour

1 cup white whole-wheat flour

1 cup granulated sugar

$\frac{1}{2}$ teaspoon salt

1 tablespoon baking soda

$\frac{1}{2}$ cup peach jam

1$\frac{1}{2}$ cups plain unsweetened almond milk

1 teaspoon lemon extract

$\frac{1}{4}$ cup fresh thyme leaves

1 cup peeled, diced peaches

1 tablespoon honey

1. Preheat oven to 400°F, and grease muffin tins with vegan margarine.
2. Combine both flours, sugar, salt, and baking soda in a large bowl. Set aside.
3. In a different large bowl, whisk together jam, milk, and lemon extract. Make sure to mix well!
4. Slowly add wet mixture to dry mixture, stirring as you pour.
5. Fold thyme into mixture, then fold peaches in gently. Add batter to muffin tins, filling each cup about $\frac{2}{3}$ of the way full.
6. Bake muffins for 25 minutes, and then cool for 10 minutes. Very gently remove muffins from tins, and drizzle with honey.

PART-TIME TIP

White whole-wheat flour is a good way to trick (yes, we're devious) your friends and family into thinking that they're not eating whole wheat. It's ground much finer than regular whole-wheat flour, which means it's smoother to the taste and touch. The King Arthur Flour brand makes a spectacular white whole-wheat baking flour.

Per Serving: 1 muffin
Calories: 148
Fat: 1 g
Protein: 3 g

Sodium: 293 mg
Fiber: 2 g
Carbohydrates: 34 g
Sugar: 17 g

WHOLE-WHEAT BRILLIANT BLUEBERRY MUFFINS

Brain food. There's a lot to be said for getting your mind running in the morning without the help of caffeine. The antioxidants in blueberries are going to keep you looking stellar and feeling fabulous. Eating one of these nutritious, filling muffins will give you some fiber and keep you away from those sugar-laden, fat-filled breakfast combos. Now *that's* a smart cookie.

YIELDS 18 MUFFINS

2 cups whole-wheat flour

1 cup white whole-wheat flour

¾ cup rolled oats

1¼ cups light brown sugar

1 tablespoon baking soda

1 teaspoon salt

1½ cups plain unsweetened almond milk

½ cup unsweetened applesauce

½ teaspoon vanilla extract

2 cups fresh blueberries

1 teaspoon powdered sugar, for garnish

1. Preheat oven to 400°F, and grease muffin tins with vegan margarine.
2. Combine flours, oats, brown sugar, baking soda, and salt in a large bowl.
3. In a second large bowl, combine milk, applesauce, and vanilla. Whisk with a fork.
4. Add wet mixture to dry mixture, then gently fold in blueberries. Pour batter into muffin tins, filling each cup about ⅔ of the way full.
5. Bake for 20 minutes. Cool for 10 minutes, and then remove muffins gently from tins. Top each muffin with a little powdered sugar and serve.

THE SKINNY ON...ALMOND MILK

There are various kinds of nondairy milk available. Soy, rice, hemp, almond—and who knows what variations people are coming up with these days? Rice milk is the thinnest, and soy milk is the most common. However, there are some excellent versions of almond milk on the store shelves these days, including Almond Breeze and Silk.

Per Serving: 1 muffin
Calories: 111
Fat: 1 g
Protein: 3 g
Sodium: 356 mg
Fiber: 3 g
Carbohydrates: 24 g
Sugar: 6 g

DOWN-HOME VEGAN BISCUITS

There is nothing like a buttered biscuit to warm your heart and have you seeing fireflies in the summer heat of the South. Smear jam on them, soak them with vegan margarine, or saturate them in honey. Let loose! Eat the whole batch if you want to.

YIELDS 12 BISCUITS

²/₃ cup plain unsweetened almond milk

1 teaspoon apple cider vinegar

2 cups whole-wheat flour

1 tablespoon baking powder

½ teaspoon salt

5 tablespoons cold vegan margarine

1. Preheat oven to 425°F.
2. Pour milk and vinegar into a small bowl. Set aside for 5 minutes to allow to curdle.
3. In a large bowl, mix flour, baking powder, and salt. Cut in cold margarine with a fork. Mix dough until it is divided into small pea-sized segments and margarine is no longer visible.
4. Add wet mixture to dry mixture, and knead by hand.
5. Sprinkle flour on a hard surface, and roll out dough until it is about ½" thick. Use a drinking glass or circle cookie cutter to cut dough into ¾" rounds. Place on an ungreased baking sheet.
6. Bake for 13 minutes until bottoms of biscuits are lightly browned.

Per Serving: 1 biscuit
Calories: 113
Fat: 5 g
Protein: 3 g
Sodium: 248 mg
Fiber: 2 g
Carbohydrates: 15 g
Sugar: 0 g

YOU SAY BANAANA, I SAY BAANANA BREAD

When you cook banana bread, make sure to use bananas that are almost ready to be thrown out. The mushier and less edible they seem, the better banana bread they'll make. This bread is moist and chewy, with a crunch that'll make you, um...go bananas.

SERVES 12

4 medium bananas, peeled

1/3 cup plain unsweetened almond milk

1 teaspoon vanilla extract

2/3 cup maple syrup

4 tablespoons cacao nibs

1/2 teaspoon apple cider vinegar

2 cups whole-wheat flour

1 teaspoon baking powder

1/2 teaspoon baking soda

1/2 teaspoon salt

1/4 teaspoon ground cinnamon

1/4 teaspoon ground nutmeg

1/4 cup raw walnuts, for garnish

1. Preheat oven to 350°F. Grease a 9" × 5" loaf pan with vegan margarine.
2. In a large bowl, mash together bananas, milk, vanilla, syrup, cacao nibs, and vinegar. Mix well.
3. In another large bowl, mix together flour, baking powder, baking soda, salt, cinnamon, and nutmeg.
4. Add banana mixture to flour mixture, mixing evenly. Pour batter into the loaf pan, and sprinkle walnuts on top.
5. Cook for 55 minutes or until a toothpick inserted into the loaf comes out clean. Let cool 10 minutes and devour.

Per Serving:
Calories: 180
Fat: 4 g
Protein: 4 g

Sodium: 188 mg
Fiber: 4 g
Carbohydrates: 37 g
Sugar: 16 g

EASY BREAKFAST BLACKBERRY BREAD PUDDING

The easiest and most delicious breakfast you'll ever make. Way more exciting than boring-beige-blasé oatmeal, and just as tasty. It's the perfect comfort breakfast food for a chilly spring morning or an autumn afternoon. Feel free to substitute any fruit you have lying around instead of the blackberries. Peach, banana, raspberries, or blueberries would all work great. You can also substitute any flavor of jam.

SERVES 1

2 slices whole-wheat bread, toasted and torn into small pieces

½ cup plain unsweetened almond milk

½ teaspoon vanilla extract

½ pint fresh blackberries

1 tablespoon honey

1 teaspoon blackberry jam

¼ teaspoon light brown sugar

1. Toss torn pieces of toast into a large un-greased stovetop pan.
2. Add milk and vanilla to the pan, and heat over medium heat so milk is warmed but not simmering, about 5 minutes.
3. Add in blackberries, honey, and jam, and continue to heat for 10 minutes until bread is saturated with milk and excess is mostly evaporated. Stir often.
4. Sprinkle with brown sugar and serve hot.

Per Serving:
Calories: 315
Fat: 4 g
Protein: 10 g

Sodium: 352 mg
Fiber: 11 g
Carbohydrates: 62 g
Sugar: 31 g

CASHEW CREAM WITH BABY TOMATOES ON MULTIGRAIN TOAST

When you're in the mood for a savory breakfast, please do stop here. Sweet can sometimes quickly turn to sickly sweet, and brunch is always best served sans sugar, if you ask us. Try out this elegant little number and convince yourself that you're royalty.

SERVES 2

2 tablespoons balsamic vinegar

½ teaspoon salt

⅛ teaspoon ground black pepper

1 pint baby tomatoes, halved

1½ cups raw cashews, soaked for 1 hour and drained

½ cup water

1½ tablespoons lemon juice

4 teaspoons apple cider vinegar

2 slices thick whole-wheat bread, toasted

¼ cup chopped fresh basil

2 tablespoons olive oil

1. In a small bowl, whisk together balsamic vinegar, salt, and black pepper. Marinate tomatoes in the mixture for 15 minutes.

2. Process cashews, water, lemon juice, and apple cider vinegar in a food processor until the consistency is creamy. The taste should be sharp and pleasant.

3. Layer each toast slice with chopped basil and marinated tomatoes. Drizzle with oil, and top with a dollop of processed cashew cream. Enjoy!

Per Serving:
Calories: 321
Fat: 21 g
Protein: 8 g

Sodium: 724 mg
Fiber: 4 g
Carbohydrates: 27 g
Sugar: 10 g

STRAWBERRY PROTEIN SMOOTHIE

A smoothie is great for those hot summer evenings when you're craving something sweet and cold, but this one won't make you curse yourself in the morning. And hey, you'll get some protein out of it! Things are always better if you can tell yourself you got protein out of it.

SERVES 2

½ cup hulled, fresh strawberries

½ (1-pound) block silken tofu

1 medium banana, peeled

¾ cup apple juice

4 ice cubes

1 tablespoon agave nectar

Combine all ingredients in a blender and blend, baby, blend.

Per Serving:
Calories: 184
Fat: 3 g
Protein: 5 g

Sodium: 10 mg
Fiber: 3 g
Carbohydrates: 37 g
Sugar: 27 g

MORNING CEREAL BARS

These bars—crunchy, sweet, and easy to be eaten on the run—don't necessarily have to be eaten in the morning. You can store them in the refrigerator until they're completely gone. Use your favorite cereal to make these bars your own.

YIELDS 12 BARS

3 cups Kashi GOLEAN Crunch cereal

1 cup all-natural peanut butter

1/3 cup Homemade Tahini (see recipe in Chapter 3)

1 cup maple syrup

1/2 teaspoon vanilla extract

2 cups muesli

1/2 cup flax meal

1/2 cup raisins

1. Grease a 9" × 13" baking pan with vegan margarine.
2. Crush cereal into small pieces. It's far less messy to do this in a medium bowl or a sealed plastic bag. Set aside.
3. In a large pot over low heat, mix peanut butter, Homemade Tahini, and syrup together for 4 minutes.
4. Remove from heat. Mix in remaining ingredients, including crushed cereal.
5. Press mixture into the greased pan, and stick it in the refrigerator for 45 minutes before cutting into squares!

PART-TIME TIP

It is crucial to store ground flax or flaxseed in the refrigerator, or else it will go rancid.

Per Serving: 1 bar
Calories: 368
Fat: 15 g
Protein: 11 g

Sodium: 88 mg
Fiber: 7 g
Carbohydrates: 54 g
Sugar: 30 g

ROSEMARY TEMPEH HASH

Less greasy than a normal hash and packed with tempeh protein. Tempeh has a naturally nutty flavor that lends itself well to the earthy flavor of the potatoes and rosemary. Yay, nature.

SERVES 4

2 medium red potatoes, boiled and diced

1 (8-ounce) package tempeh, diced

2 tablespoons olive oil

2 scallions, chopped

1 tablespoon chili powder

1 teaspoon dried rosemary leaves

1/8 teaspoon salt

1/8 teaspoon ground black pepper

1. In a large saucepan over medium heat, sauté potatoes and tempeh in oil for 3 minutes.
2. Add remaining ingredients to the pan. Stir and cook for another 4 minutes. Voilà!

Per Serving:
Calories: 252
Fat: 13 g
Protein: 14 g

Sodium: 157 mg
Fiber: 3 g
Carbohydrates: 23 g
Sugar: 2 g

CHILI MASALA TOFU SCRAMBLE

Scrambling tofu is a great way to recreate the taste and texture of scrambled eggs. It's great as leftovers too! Eat this in a sandwich for a brunch. Make some vegan pancakes, pour a fresh glass of almond milk...and you'll be ready for anything.

SERVES 4

1 small onion, peeled and diced

2 cloves garlic, peeled and minced

2 tablespoons olive oil

1 (1-pound) block firm tofu, pressed and cut into 1"-thick cubes

1 small red chili, seeded and minced

1 medium green bell pepper, seeded and chopped

¾ cup sliced white mushrooms

1 tablespoon soy sauce

1 teaspoon curry powder

½ teaspoon ground cumin

¼ teaspoon ground turmeric

1 teaspoon nutritional yeast

1. Sauté onion and garlic in oil in a large pan for 2 minutes over medium heat.
2. Add tofu, chili, bell pepper, and mushrooms. Stir to mix everything well.
3. Add remaining ingredients except nutritional yeast. Stir mixture until tofu is browned, about 8 minutes.
4. Remove from heat, sprinkle with nutritional yeast, and serve.

PART-TIME TIP

There are lots of variations on a tofu scramble! Think of your favorite combos. Try spinach and broccoli, vegan cheese and tomato, or a spicy southwestern tofu take on huevos rancheros.

Per Serving:
Calories: 128
Fat: 5 g
Protein: 12 g

Sodium: 261 mg
Fiber: 3 g
Carbohydrates: 9 g
Sugar: 3 g

CHAPTER 3

DIPS, SNACKS, AND APPETIZERS

THAT SHALL IMPRESS YOUR FRIENDS

PURELY VEGAN CHOCOLATE HAZELNUT SPREAD

Sometimes the thought of giving up some of your favorite foods is just too much to bear. How can you live without a Hershey's chocolate bar or bread and butter? Luckily, there always seems to be a vegan way around these things! This version of chocolate hazelnut spread is not only delicious but also cuts down on the sugar and is good for you! It'll be love at first bite.

YIELDS 2 CUPS

2 cups shelled hazelnuts

1 cup plain unsweetened almond milk

2 teaspoons vanilla extract

3 tablespoons canola oil

½ cup dark cocoa powder (Hershey's brand works great)

1 cup powdered sugar

1. Process hazelnuts until they are a fine meal or until mixture begins to stick to the side of the food processor and won't mix any longer. This may take a few minutes. Be careful not to overheat your processor!
2. Add milk, vanilla, and oil, and blend until combined.
3. Add cocoa and sugar. You can add more sugar depending on your tastes! Keep blending until smooth. Store for up to 5 days in a tightly sealed container in the refrigerator.

PART-TIME TIP

It takes a strong and sturdy food processor with the heart and soul of a tiger to convert any nut into a nut butter. Don't worry if yours is not this adventurous: We've designed this recipe to work with any old food processor. If the situation gets sticky, you can always add a dash more canola oil or some almond milk to loosen things up.

Per Serving: 2 tbsp
Calories: 120
Fat: 9 g
Protein: 2 g

Sodium: 9 mg
Fiber: 2 g
Carbohydrates: 8 g
Sugar: 6 g

QUICK, HOMEMADE, RAW VEGAN PESTO

Traditional pesto is made using pine nuts, but pine nuts seem to be members of a club that is exclusively expensive and posh. Luckily you can easily substitute walnuts or even almonds for pine nuts. The pesto tastes great, and people will never know you swindled them. Which is exactly what we're going for, isn't it?

YIELDS 1½ CUPS

- 1 cup raw walnuts
- ½ cup olive oil
- ½ teaspoon salt
- 4 cloves garlic, peeled and minced
- 3 packed cups fresh basil leaves
- 1 teaspoon ground black pepper
- ½ cup lemon juice
- 1 tablespoon nutritional yeast

Process all ingredients in a food processor until fragrant and well blended. Watch out for the salt, which can overpower the flavor of the basil if you are tempted to add more than ½ teaspoon.

THE SKINNY ON...NUTRITIONAL YEAST

Apart from having the most unappealing food name ever, nutritional yeast is a powerhouse of B vitamins and protein. Many people are initially turned off by its sharp, "cheese"-like flavor, but give it a chance! To start, try sprinkling a little on top of popcorn or over some lettuce with a little olive oil, salt, and pepper.

Per Serving: ¼ cup
Calories: 227
Fat: 23 g
Protein: 3 g

Sodium: 148 mg
Fiber: 1 g
Carbohydrates: 4 g
Sugar: 1 g

EASY BROCCOLI SNACK ATTACK

For when you have the munchies at midnight and your old love, the bag of chips, is texting your phone nonstop. Fiber up. You can basically eat a whole bag of broccoli by yourself and consume only about 100 calories. Good calories! Cut things off with the potato chips: opportunity is ringing!

SERVES 1

1 (1-pound) bag frozen broccoli, defrosted and cut into fine pieces

1 tablespoon nutritional yeast

1 teaspoon garlic powder

1 tablespoon lemon juice

⅛ teaspoon salt

⅛ teaspoon ground black pepper

Top cut broccoli with remaining ingredients and mix well. Enjoy!

Per Serving:
Calories: 148
Fat: 1 g
Protein: 16 g

Sodium: 346 mg
Fiber: 14 g
Carbohydrates: 28 g
Sugar: 7 g

QUICK GARLIC, ZUCCHINI, EGGPLANT, AND ONION SPREAD

The best veggies to combine together. The result is so mouthwatering and luscious. The natural flavors of all these vegetables are the perfect complements to one another. This dish makes a great party spread for a chopped-up baguette.

SERVES 4

- 6 cloves garlic, peeled and minced
- 4 medium zucchini, chopped
- 1 medium eggplant, chopped
- 1 medium yellow onion, peeled and finely chopped
- 1 tablespoon red wine vinegar
- 4 tablespoons olive oil
- 1/8 teaspoon salt
- 1/8 teaspoon ground black pepper
- 2 teaspoons nutritional yeast

In a large saucepan, combine all ingredients. Cook over low heat, stirring continuously, for 15 minutes until completely soft and mixed. Serve hot as a spread!

Per Serving:
Calories: 208
Fat: 14 g
Protein: 5 g

Sodium: 95 mg
Fiber: 6 g
Carbohydrates: 18 g
Sugar: 10 g

BAKED ZUCCHINI FRIES

Try not to thank yourself after you bake this incredible french fry substitute. Really, should we even call it a substitute? How about new, fantastic, love of your life? These fries mimic your traditional fast-food favorites, but they are also healthy, crunchy, and packed with the nutritional benefits of olive oil. Heart-stopping—in a good way.

SERVES 2

½ cup whole-wheat flour

½ teaspoon peeled, minced garlic

½ teaspoon paprika

½ teaspoon onion powder

⅛ teaspoon salt

⅛ teaspoon ground black pepper

1 tablespoon nutritional yeast

2 medium zucchini, cut into 2" strips

¼ cup olive oil

1. Preheat oven to 450°F.
2. Mix flour, garlic, paprika, onion powder, salt, pepper, and nutritional yeast in a small bowl. Set aside.
3. Brush zucchini strips with a very light coating of olive oil.
4. Toss fries into the bowl with flour seasoning mix. After they are coated, place them on an ungreased baking sheet.
5. Lightly brush coated fries with olive oil once more, and bake for 15 minutes. Serve with marinara or vegan "Alfredo" sauce!

Per Serving:
Calories: 386
Fat: 29 g
Protein: 7 g

Sodium: 166 mg
Fiber: 6 g
Carbohydrates: 29 g
Sugar: 5 g

EASY HUMMUS

Hummus. Packed with protein. Creamy and delicious. Use it on sandwiches, crackers, or toast! Or, you know, just eat it from the bowl. Plain. As an entire meal.

YIELDS 1½ CUPS

- 1 (15-ounce) can chickpeas, undrained
- 2 tablespoons Homemade Tahini (see recipe in this chapter)
- 2 tablespoons olive oil
- ¾ teaspoon salt
- 2 teaspoons lemon juice
- 2 teaspoons peeled, minced garlic
- ¼ cup chopped cherry tomatoes, for garnish
- ½ tablespoon olive oil, for garnish
- ⅛ teaspoon paprika, for garnish

Simply process all ingredients, except garnishes, together in a food processor. Top hummus with chopped cherry tomatoes, olive oil, and paprika!

THE SKINNY ON...LACTYLATE

Lots of breads that you may use for toast, dipping, and so forth have an ingredient called lactylate (or sodium stearoyl lactylate). It's a food additive used to blend ingredients that don't normally blend (such as oil and water), and it can be synthetic, plant-based, or animal-derived. This is one of those ingredients that can turn a seemingly vegan item non-vegan.

Per Serving: 2 tbsp
Calories: 49
Fat: 3 g
Protein: 1 g

Sodium: 163 mg
Fiber: 1 g
Carbohydrates: 4 g
Sugar: 0 g

LEAN, MEAN, BLACK BEAN GUACAMOLE

Sometimes you just can't improve an old favorite. This is not one of those times. Adding black beans to guac is a way to change up your old standby without casting him off as just a bygone lover. Think of it as a fiber-rich, protein-adding makeover for your favorite Mexican dip.

YIELDS 2 CUPS

- 1 (15-ounce) can black beans, partially drained
- 3 medium avocados, peeled and pitted
- 1 tablespoon lemon juice
- ¼ cup chopped fresh cilantro
- ½ medium red onion, peeled and diced
- 1 large tomato, diced
- 2 cloves garlic, peeled and chopped
- ¼ teaspoon chili powder
- ¼ teaspoon ground cumin
- ¼ teaspoon salt

1. Using a fork, mash beans in a large bowl. Don't turn them into mush, but rather leave some texture.
2. Mix remaining ingredients into the bowl with beans.
3. Store covered in the refrigerator until ready to serve! You can save the scrumptious leftovers for up to 3 days in the refrigerator.

Per Serving: 2 tbsp
Calories: 33
Fat: 2 g
Protein: 1 g

Sodium: 29 mg
Fiber: 2 g
Carbohydrates: 3 g
Sugar: 0 g

MANGO CITRUS SALSA

Picture this: you, squinting from the bright and brilliant sun, standing on the warm sand in front of crystalline waters and watching the turquoise waves drop and pull away. The heady, floral caress of wind in the palm trees and your hair. A cold drink in one hand. And with the other: delicate fingers grasping a chip, plunging it into this cool, refreshing salsa. Paradise is one bite away.

YIELDS 2 CUPS

1 medium mango, peeled and chopped

2 medium tangerines, peeled and chopped

½ medium red bell pepper, seeded and chopped

½ medium red onion, peeled and minced

3 cloves garlic, peeled and minced

½ medium jalapeño pepper, seeded and minced

2 tablespoons lime juice

½ teaspoon salt

½ teaspoon cayenne pepper

½ teaspoon ground black pepper

3 tablespoons chopped fresh cilantro

1. Mix all ingredients together in a large bowl.
2. Let mixture sit for 15 minutes to allow the flavors to meet and greet, then serve!

Per Serving: 2 tbsp
Calories: 16
Fat: 0 g
Protein: 0 g

Sodium: 52 mg
Fiber: 1 g
Carbohydrates: 4 g
Sugar: 3 g

ROASTED CHICKPEAS, PLEASE

Crunchy. Tasty. Feels like you're eating a snack that should be bad for you but somehow is suspiciously good for you. All in a day's work!

SERVES 2

2 (15-ounce) cans chickpeas, drained

2 teaspoons ground cumin

1 teaspoon salt

1 teaspoon ground black pepper

1 teaspoon peeled, minced garlic

1 teaspoon paprika

1 teaspoon ground turmeric

1. Preheat oven to 450°F.
2. Season chickpeas with spices, and spread them evenly onto an ungreased baking sheet.
3. Cook for approximately 45 minutes, mixing once halfway through cooking. Let cool for 5 minutes before eating.

Per Serving:
Calories: 202
Fat: 4 g
Protein: 10 g

Sodium: 1,492 mg
Fiber: 10 g
Carbohydrates: 33 g
Sugar: 5 g

TROPICAL CASHEW NUT BUTTER

You can make a homemade cashew nut butter with any kind of oil, so feel free to substitute using whatever you have on hand, but you're in for a real treat when you use coconut oil in this recipe!

MAKES ¾ CUP

2 cups roasted cashews

½ teaspoon sugar

¼ teaspoon salt

4 tablespoons coconut oil

1. Process cashews, sugar, and salt in a food processor on high speed until finely ground. Continue processing until cashews form a thick paste.
2. Slowly add coconut oil until smooth and creamy, scraping down sides as you process.

Per Serving: 2 tbsp
Calories: 187
Fat: 16 g
Protein: 4 g

Sodium: 56 mg
Fiber: 1 g
Carbohydrates: 8 g
Sugar: 1 g

(YOU'RE) HOT ARTICHOKE SPINACH DIP

Traditional spinach dips are loaded with calories and unforgiving fats. Luckily for all of us, this version combines all of the creaminess and flavor of the original with "cheesy" goodness, vegan-style. Spread it onto some store-bought mini toasts or some toasted pita bread. You'll impress your guests, and your waist will thank you.

SERVES 8

1 (12-ounce) package frozen spinach, thawed

1 (14-ounce) can artichoke hearts, drained

¼ cup vegan margarine, such as Earth Balance

¼ cup whole-wheat flour

2 cups plain unsweetened almond milk

½ cup nutritional yeast

1 teaspoon garlic powder

1½ teaspoons onion powder

½ teaspoon ground white pepper

¼ teaspoon salt

1. Preheat oven to 350°F.
2. Purée spinach and artichokes together in a food processor, and set aside.
3. In a medium saucepan over medium heat, melt margarine for 30 seconds, and spoon in flour 1 tablespoon at a time. Keep stirring slowly until mixture thickens, about 5 minutes. Remove from heat.
4. In a large bowl, combine margarine mix, artichoke and spinach purée, and remaining ingredients. Place mixture in an ungreased 9"× 13" oven-safe dish, and bake uncovered for 20 minutes. Serve hot!

THE SKINNY ON...VEGAN MARGARINE

Most margarines are in fact vegan in the sense that they use no animal-derived products. However, they may be manufactured in places where milk products are dealt with, so potentially they could have been "contaminated" with whey or lactose. If you are looking for 100 percent certified vegan margarine, just check the labels.

Per Serving:
Calories: 114
Fat: 7 g
Protein: 5 g

Sodium: 305 mg
Fiber: 3 g
Carbohydrates: 9 g
Sugar: 1 g

PARSLEY AND ONION DIP

Be prepared to get addicted. This tangy, lively dip is going to be the hit of your party. Dip pretzels into it, veggies, crisps, chips—heck, a spoon works too. People will have no idea it's missing the fat-laden sour cream that is usually the main ingredient of onion dips. But *you* won't be missing it at all. Clever minx.

SERVES 6

1 medium yellow onion, peeled and chopped

3 cloves garlic, peeled and minced

1 tablespoon olive oil

1 (1-pound) block firm tofu, well pressed

½ teaspoon onion powder

3 teaspoons lemon juice

1 teaspoon apple cider vinegar

¼ cup chopped fresh Italian flat-leaf parsley

2 tablespoons chopped fresh chives

¼ teaspoon salt

1. In a large saucepan, sauté onion and garlic in oil for about 4 minutes over medium heat. Make sure onions are soft and slightly translucent. Remove from heat, and let mixture cool.

2. Process onion and garlic mixture along with tofu, onion powder, and lemon juice in a food processor.

3. Spoon mixture into a large bowl, and mix in remaining ingredients manually. Consider it your exercise for the day. Serve immediately, or store covered in the refrigerator for up to 2 days.

THE SKINNY ON...PRESSING TOFU

Pressing tofu drains it of extra water. This allows it to be drier, denser, and more able to absorb flavor. Simply lay the tofu on a couple of paper towels, hand-pressing another paper towel on the top of the tofu to remove visible water. Next, replace all paper towels and set a heavy object (such as a can) on top of the tofu for 20 minutes.

Per Serving:
Calories: 96
Fat: 6 g
Protein: 7 g

Sodium: 103 mg
Fiber: 1 g
Carbohydrates: 4 g
Sugar: 1 g

HOMEMADE TAHINI

We've made quick-and-easy hummus, but one of the ingredients, tahini paste, is a bit on the expensive side. Here's a recipe for homemade tahini to use in your homemade hummus—very pioneering of you. You can also use tahini as an ingredient in a salad dressing or even as a dip by itself. Add ½ teaspoon paprika, ¼ teaspoon salt, and ½ teaspoon ground black pepper if using as a stand-alone dip.

YIELDS 1 CUP

2 cups sesame seeds

½ cup olive oil

1. Preheat oven to 350°F.
2. Lay sesame seeds on an ungreased baking sheet, and bake for 6 minutes. Make sure to stir them once halfway through baking.
3. After seeds cool down, throw them into a food processor with oil, making sure to get the consistency as creamy as possible. If your food processor is throwing a conniption and the tahini isn't coming out creamy, add a tiny bit more oil.

Per Serving: 2 tbsp
Calories: 196
Fat: 19 g
Protein: 4 g

Sodium: 46 mg
Fiber: 3 g
Carbohydrates: 5 g
Sugar: 0 g

NACHO "CHEESE" DIP

You won't miss those dubious-looking canned and artificial cheese dips once you cook up this delicious recipe. Top with some guacamole, and dip in your favorite tortilla chips. Then, of course, snack away!

SERVES 4

3 tablespoons vegan margarine

1 cup unsweetened soy milk

¾ teaspoon onion powder

½ teaspoon garlic powder

½ teaspoon salt

1 tablespoon all-natural peanut butter

¼ cup whole-wheat flour

¼ cup nutritional yeast

¾ cup Mango Citrus Salsa (see recipe in this chapter)

2 tablespoons seeded, chopped jalapeños

1. In a medium saucepan, heat margarine and milk for 30 seconds over low heat. Add in onion powder, garlic powder, and salt. Drop in peanut butter, and stir well until everything is combined.

2. Add flour into mixture 1 tablespoon at a time. Stir continuously until thickened, about 5 minutes.

3. Add nutritional yeast, Mango Citrus Salsa, and jalapeños. Remove from heat, and let cool for 10 minutes. The dip will thicken up more as it cools off. Serve warm.

Per Serving:
Calories: 199
Fat: 12 g
Protein: 6 g

Sodium: 498 mg
Fiber: 3 g
Carbohydrates: 18 g
Sugar: 7 g

VEGAN "PIGS" IN A BLANKET

Bite-sized popular appetizers go vegan. So easy to make and perfect alongside spicy mustard or plain old ketchup.

SERVES 8

1 batch Down-Home Vegan Biscuits dough (see recipe in Chapter 2)

8 vegan hot dogs, sliced in half

1. Preheat oven to 400°F. Lightly grease a baking sheet with vegan margarine.
2. Divide dough into 8 balls and roll each one out.
3. Place a hot dog into the center of each rolled-out dough ball, and roll up.
4. Place hot dogs on the baking sheet, and cook for 12 minutes.

Per Serving:
Calories: 219
Fat: 8 g
Protein: 11 g

Sodium: 803 mg
Fiber: 4 g
Carbohydrates: 27 g
Sugar: 2 g

VEGAN CHEESE BALL

Serve with delicate little crackers for a truly elegant display. It will be ever so lovely. Do remember to give yourself a pat on the back. Good show! By George. Carry on!

YIELDS 1 LARGE CHEESE BALL OR 14 BITE-SIZED CHEESE BALLS

1 (8-ounce) block vegan Cheddar cheese, room temperature, finely grated

1 (12-ounce) container vegan cream cheese

1 teaspoon garlic powder

½ teaspoon hot sauce

¼ teaspoon salt

1 teaspoon paprika

¼ cup finely chopped raw walnuts

1. Mash grated cheese together with cream cheese, garlic powder, hot sauce, and salt in a large bowl. Chill covered for 1 hour until firm.
2. Shape mixture into a log. Sprinkle with paprika and roll in walnuts.

Per Serving: 1 small ball
Calories: 126
Fat: 12 g
Protein: 3 g
Sodium: 247 mg
Fiber: 2 g
Carbohydrates: 4 g
Sugar: 1 g

EGGPLANT BABA GHANOUSH

A traditional Middle Eastern spread, this dip will be an adventure for those who've never tried it. Creamy with a tang, it's the perfect topper for pita bread or buttery crackers.

SERVES 4

- 2 medium eggplants, halved and pricked with a fork
- 3 tablespoons olive oil, divided
- 2 tablespoons lemon juice
- ¼ cup Homemade Tahini (see recipe in this chapter)
- 3 cloves garlic, peeled
- ½ teaspoon ground cumin
- ½ teaspoon chili powder
- ¼ teaspoon salt
- 1 tablespoon chopped fresh Italian flat-leaf parsley

1. Preheat oven to 400°F.
2. Drizzle eggplant with 1 tablespoon oil, and then bake for 30 minutes on an ungreased baking sheet.
3. Scoop out eggplant insides and place them in a large bowl. Mash eggplant together with remaining ingredients. Serve warm.

Per Serving:
Calories: 263
Fat: 20 g
Protein: 5 g

Sodium: 185 mg
Fiber: 9 g
Carbohydrates: 20 g
Sugar: 9 g

EASY FRIED TOFU

In this case it's all in the name, folks. An easy, tasty dish that you can munch on as a snack when the 3:00 p.m. hunger monster creeps up on you. With this, you shall defeat him valiantly.

SERVES 3

1 (1-pound) block extra-firm tofu, cubed

¼ cup soy sauce

2 tablespoons whole-wheat flour

2 tablespoons nutritional yeast

1 teaspoon garlic powder

¼ teaspoon salt

⅛ teaspoon ground black pepper

1 teaspoon canola oil

1. Marinate tofu in soy sauce in a small covered bowl for 1 hour.
2. Mix flour, nutritional yeast, garlic powder, salt, and pepper together in a medium bowl. Coat pieces of tofu in flour mixture.
3. In a medium skillet over medium heat, heat oil for 30 seconds, then fry tofu for 5 minutes on both sides until golden. (And you thought fried food was bad for you.)

Per Serving:
Calories: 206
Fat: 10 g
Protein: 20 g

Sodium: 1,546 mg
Fiber: 3 g
Carbohydrates: 11 g
Sugar: 1 g

SINLESS TVP CHILI "CHEESE" FRIES

Oh, it's soooo tough being a vegan. Vegans can't eat anything. Except for chili cheese fries.

SERVES 4

1 (20-ounce) bag frozen french fries

1½ cups TVP

2 cups hot water

½ medium yellow onion, peeled and chopped

1 tablespoon olive oil

1 (15-ounce) can kidney beans, drained

1½ cups tomato paste

2 tablespoons chili powder

½ teaspoon ground cumin

½ teaspoon cayenne pepper

2 tablespoons vegan margarine

2 tablespoons whole-wheat flour

1½ cups unsweetened soy milk

2 tablespoons yellow mustard

½ teaspoon garlic powder

½ teaspoon salt

½ cup grated vegan cheese

1. Cook fries using the instructions on the packaging.
2. Rehydrate TVP by combining it with hot water in a large bowl. Let sit for 7 minutes, then drain.
3. In a medium saucepan over medium heat, cook onion in oil for 3 minutes until translucent. Reduce heat to medium-low and add TVP, beans, tomato paste, chili powder, cumin, and cayenne pepper. Cover and cook for 10 minutes.
4. In another medium pan over low heat, melt margarine for 30 seconds, then add flour to form a paste. Stir in milk, mustard, garlic powder, and salt. Add cheese and stir. Heat until everything is fully mixed about 2 minutes.
5. Top fries with TVP chili, followed by "cheese" sauce.

Per Serving:
Calories: 695
Fat: 27 g
Protein: 33 g

Sodium: 1,404 mg
Fiber: 17 g
Carbohydrates: 83 g
Sugar: 14 g

SEITAN BUFFALO WINGS

Buffalo sauce is the most delicious thing on earth. On the whole entire earth. Buffalo themselves may be a little confused, but that doesn't particularly matter at this juncture. These wings are spicy and the ideal snack while watching (insert Sport of Choice here).

SERVES 4

⅓ cup vegan margarine

⅓ cup Louisiana hot sauce

1 cup whole-wheat flour

1 teaspoon garlic powder

1 teaspoon onion powder

¼ teaspoon ground black pepper

½ cup unsweetened soy milk

1 (16-ounce) package seitan

1 teaspoon canola oil

1. In a small saucepan over low heat, add margarine and hot sauce. Stir 30 seconds until margarine is melted. Set buffalo sauce aside.

2. In a small bowl, combine flour, garlic powder, onion powder, and pepper. Add milk to a second small bowl. Dip seitan in milk, then flour mixture. Set coated seitan aside.

3. In a deep saucepan over medium heat, heat oil for 30 seconds. Fry seitan in oil for 5 minutes until brown, making sure to cook all sides. Transfer to a serving plate.

4. Cover cooked seitan in buffalo sauce, dip into a ranch dressing of your choosing, and go to town!

Per Serving:
Calories: 391
Fat: 17 g
Protein: 26 g

Sodium: 634 mg
Fiber: 5 g
Carbohydrates: 36 g
Sugar: 3 g

CRISPY TEMPEH FRIES

These fries are absolutely delicious for a snack with marinara sauce or bean dip, or all on their own. You can also sprinkle a little nutritional yeast over these or some melted vegan shredded cheese and "fakeon"—that is, fake bacon. It's not a crime to have a little throwback to the days of meat and fatty cheese every now and then.

SERVES 2

1 (8-ounce) package tempeh, sliced into thin strips

½ teaspoon salt

½ teaspoon chili powder

½ teaspoon garlic powder

⅔ cup canola oil

1. Simmer tempeh in water over medium-low heat for about 10 minutes to soften. Drain excess liquid.
2. While tempeh pieces are still wet, sprinkle them with salt, chili powder, and garlic powder.
3. In a medium saucepan, heat oil for 30 seconds over medium-low heat. Fry tempeh pieces for 6 minutes in oil until browned and crispy. Let them cool for 30 minutes on a paper towel (to absorb excess oil).
4. After pieces cool, heat oil once more for 30 seconds, then fry tempeh again for 6 minutes.

Per Serving:
Calories: 275
Fat: 18 g
Protein: 23 g

Sodium: 611 mg
Fiber: 0 g
Carbohydrates: 10 g
Sugar: 0 g

CHAPTER 4

SALADS AND SALAD DRESSINGS

THAT ARE EASIER THAN PIE

CUCUMBER CILANTRO SALAD

This is a very refreshing, simple salad to make. Mixing the freshness of cucumbers with the creaminess of yogurt is both satisfying and light. Use this to cool you off on a hot day, and pair it with a glass of white wine.

SERVES 2

4 medium cucumbers, diced

2 medium tomatoes, chopped

1/2 medium red onion, peeled and diced small

1 cup plain soy yogurt

1 tablespoon lemon juice

2 tablespoons chopped fresh cilantro

1/2 teaspoon cayenne pepper

1/8 teaspoon salt

Simply toss all ingredients together in a large bowl, stir, and chill covered in the refrigerator for 2 hours. Toss once more before serving.

Per Serving:
Calories: 206
Fat: 3 g
Protein: 9 g

Sodium: 181 mg
Fiber: 6 g
Carbohydrates: 42 g
Sugar: 21 g

EDAMAME SALAD

Edamame will save your life. Keep a bag of it around for meals, snacks, late-night binges, breakfast, lunch, brunch, or sleepwalking. It is a delicious and healthy treat, easy to cook, easy to eat, and easy to clean up. Basically it's too incredible to describe properly—like you, dear reader.

SERVES 4

- 2 cups frozen shelled edamame, thawed and drained
- 1 medium red bell pepper, seeded and diced
- 2 tablespoons chopped fresh cilantro
- 2 tablespoons olive oil
- 2 tablespoons red wine vinegar
- 1 teaspoon soy sauce
- 1 teaspoon chili powder
- 2 teaspoons lemon juice
- 1/8 teaspoon salt
- 1/8 teaspoon ground black pepper

1. In a medium bowl, mix edamame, bell pepper, and cilantro.
2. In a different medium bowl, whisk together remaining ingredients. Pour mixture over edamame.
3. Allow mixture to sit covered in the refrigerator for 1 hour before serving. The beans will absorb the flavor and be delicious.

Per Serving:
Calories: 168
Fat: 11 g
Protein: 10 g

Sodium: 183 mg
Fiber: 5 g
Carbohydrates: 9 g
Sugar: 3 g

VEGAN POTATO PESTO SALAD

Were you addicted to egg or potato salad before you decided to give veganism a try? Think nothing could ever replace it? Think again. This potato salad, served cold, is creamy, zesty, and perfect for a picnic either outside or on the living room floor—your choice.

SERVES 4

- ¼ cup Italian dressing or Old Reliable: Balsamic Vinaigrette (see recipe in this chapter)
- ¼ cup Vegan Mayonnaise (see recipe in this chapter)
- ½ cup Quick, Homemade, Raw Vegan Pesto (see recipe in Chapter 3)
- 1 medium red bell pepper, seeded and chopped
- ½ medium red onion, peeled and chopped
- 2 pounds red potatoes, cooked and diced
- ¼ cup chopped fresh Italian flat-leaf parsley
- ⅓ cup sliced black olives
- ⅛ teaspoon salt
- ⅛ teaspoon ground black pepper

1. Mix together dressing and Vegan Mayonnaise in a small bowl.
2. Combine all remaining ingredients in a large bowl. Pour ingredients from the small bowl into the large bowl. Mix and refrigerate covered until ready to serve.

Per Serving:
Calories: 379
Fat: 20 g
Protein: 7 g

Sodium: 389 mg
Fiber: 6 g
Carbohydrates: 45 g
Sugar: 7 g

LEAN, MEAN, KIDNEY BEAN AND CHICKPEA SALAD

Full of fiber and packed with protein, kidney beans and chickpeas are the perfect complement to a light, tangy, vinegar-based marinade. This salad is a great side dish for vegan ribs (yep, those exist; look for them in the vegan frozen section) or corn bread.

SERVES 6

¼ cup olive oil

¼ cup red wine vinegar

½ teaspoon paprika

2 tablespoons lemon juice

1 (14-ounce) can chickpeas, drained

1 (14-ounce) can dark red kidney beans, drained

½ cup sliced black olives

1 (8-ounce) can corn, drained

½ medium red onion, peeled and chopped

1 tablespoon chopped fresh Italian flat-leaf parsley

⅛ teaspoon salt

⅛ teaspoon ground black pepper

1. Whisk together oil, vinegar, paprika, and lemon juice in a small bowl.
2. Combine remaining ingredients in a large bowl, mixing thoroughly. Pour oil mixture over top. Mix again.
3. Let mixture sit for 30 minutes, either in the refrigerator or at room temperature. Serve.

Per Serving:
Calories: 229
Fat: 12 g
Protein: 7 g

Sodium: 327 mg
Fiber: 6 g
Carbohydrates: 24 g
Sugar: 4 g

SOY AND SESAME COLESLAW SALAD

Forget the mayo. This coleslaw gets its flavor from soy sauce and maple syrup. Throw a little tofu in to make a complete meal.

SERVES 4

- 1 medium head Napa cabbage, shredded
- 1 medium carrot, peeled and grated
- 2 scallions, chopped
- 1 medium red bell pepper, seeded and sliced thin
- 2 tablespoons olive oil
- 2 tablespoons apple cider vinegar
- 2 teaspoons soy sauce
- ½ teaspoon sesame oil
- 2 tablespoons maple syrup
- 2 tablespoons sesame seeds

1. Mix cabbage, carrot, scallions, and bell pepper in a large bowl. Set aside.
2. In a small bowl, whisk together remaining ingredients except sesame seeds. Drizzle over cabbage mixture. Top with sesame seeds and serve.

Per Serving:
Calories: 171
Fat: 10 g
Protein: 5 g

Sodium: 218 mg
Fiber: 3 g
Carbohydrates: 19 g
Sugar: 12 g

DELI-STYLE MACARONI SALAD

This pasta salad is made using Vegan Mayonnaise (see recipe in this chapter). Make sure to salt the water generously when you cook the pasta! This is the secret to making it delicious and rich.

SERVES 6

- 2 cups cooked whole-wheat macaroni
- 1 medium carrot, peeled and diced small
- ½ cup frozen green peas, thawed
- ½ cup frozen corn, thawed
- 1 rib celery, diced
- ½ cup Vegan Mayonnaise (see recipe in this chapter)
- 1½ tablespoons yellow mustard
- 2 tablespoons apple cider vinegar
- 2 tablespoons sweet pickle relish
- 2 teaspoons granulated sugar
- 1 tablespoon chopped fresh dill
- ⅛ teaspoon salt
- ⅛ teaspoon ground black pepper

1. In a large bowl, mix together macaroni, carrot, peas, corn, and celery.
2. In a medium bowl, mix together Vegan Mayonnaise, mustard, vinegar, relish, and sugar. Stir in dill, salt, and pepper.
3. Add mayonnaise mixture to macaroni mixture and stir together. Chill covered in the refrigerator for 2 hours, and serve!

Per Serving:
Calories: 135
Fat: 4 g
Protein: 4 g

Sodium: 208 mg
Fiber: 3 g
Carbohydrates: 22 g
Sugar: 5 g

HOT GERMAN DIJON POTATO SALAD

Do you ever have those days when you say, "Man, I really feel like a hot German Dijon potato salad?" Yeah, didn't think so. But you will in the future if you try this recipe.

SERVES 4

- ½ medium yellow onion, peeled and sliced thin
- 2 tablespoons olive oil
- ⅓ cup water
- ⅓ cup white vinegar
- 1 tablespoon Dijon mustard
- 1 tablespoon whole-wheat flour
- 1 teaspoon granulated sugar
- 4 large red potatoes, cooked, cooled, and cut into ½" cubes
- 2 scallions, chopped
- ⅛ teaspoon salt
- ⅛ teaspoon ground black pepper

1. In a medium saucepan over medium-high heat, sauté onion in oil for 3 minutes. Add water, vinegar, mustard, flour, and sugar. Stir. Simmer 1 minute to thicken mixture.
2. Lower the heat, and add potatoes and scallions. Stir for 3 minutes until mixture is heated through. Season with salt and pepper, and serve!

Per Serving:
Calories: 345
Fat: 7 g
Protein: 8 g

Sodium: 232 mg
Fiber: 7 g
Carbohydrates: 63 g
Sugar: 7 g

LEMON CUMIN POTATO SALAD

An unexpected twist on traditional potato salad. Somebody hold us back before it's too late.

SERVES 4

1 small yellow onion, peeled and sliced

2 tablespoons olive oil

4 large red potatoes, cooked, cooled, and chopped

1½ teaspoons ground cumin

3 tablespoons lemon juice

2 teaspoons Dijon mustard

1 scallion, chopped

¼ teaspoon cayenne pepper

2 tablespoons chopped fresh cilantro

1. In a large saucepan over medium-high heat, sauté onion in oil for 3 minutes.
2. Stir in potatoes and cumin. Cook for 1 minute, then remove from heat quickly so nothing burns.
3. Whisk together remaining ingredients in a small bowl and pour over potato mixture, stirring well.
4. Chill covered in the refrigerator for 1 hour, then serve!

Per Serving:
Calories: 339
Fat: 7 g
Protein: 8 g

Sodium: 130 mg
Fiber: 7 g
Carbohydrates: 63 g
Sugar: 6 g

77

CARROT AND DATE SALAD

The natural sweetness of carrots and encouraging saccharine flavor of dates meld together perfectly in this salad. The citrus island flavor of this recipe is perfect for a picnic or a day at the beach—or to add a little sunshine into your soul.

SERVES 6

1 tablespoon olive oil

2 tablespoons agave nectar

3 tablespoons lemon juice

¼ teaspoon salt

4 large carrots, peeled and grated

½ cup pitted, chopped dates

3 medium mandarin oranges, peeled and sectioned

⅓ cup coconut flakes

1. Whisk together oil, agave nectar, lemon juice, and salt in a large bowl.
2. Add carrots to oil mixture and mix well. Stir in dates, oranges, and coconut. Let sit 1 hour before serving.

Per Serving:
Calories: 143
Fat: 5 g
Protein: 1 g

Sodium: 132 mg
Fiber: 4 g
Carbohydrates: 25 g
Sugar: 19 g

TANGERINE AND MINT SALAD

A simple salad for two that you can throw together when you want something that isn't just your typical greens. Cracked red pepper lends a delicious and soft pepper flavor—as well as a pretty garnish—to this salad. If you can't find any, black pepper works just as well, of course.

SERVES 2

- 1 medium head green lettuce, chopped
- 2 tablespoons chopped fresh mint
- 2 medium tangerines, peeled and sectioned
- 1/3 cup chopped raw walnuts
- 2 tablespoons olive oil
- 1/8 teaspoon salt
- 1/8 teaspoon fresh cracked red pepper

Simply toss together lettuce, mint, tangerines, and walnuts in a large bowl, top with oil, and season with salt and pepper.

Per Serving:
Calories: 310
Fat: 27 g
Protein: 6 g

Sodium: 198 mg
Fiber: 5 g
Carbohydrates: 17 g
Sugar: 9 g

EGGLESS "EGG" SALAD

This recipe is just so *cool*. Seriously, it's eggless—yet it tastes exactly like egg salad.

SERVES 4

1 (1-pound) block firm tofu

1 (1-pound) block silken tofu

$\frac{1}{2}$ cup Vegan Mayonnaise (see recipe in this chapter)

$\frac{1}{3}$ cup sweet pickle relish

$\frac{3}{4}$ teaspoon apple cider vinegar

2 tablespoons dried minced onion

$1\frac{1}{2}$ tablespoons Dijon mustard

2 tablespoons chopped fresh chives

1 tablespoon chopped fresh dill

1 teaspoon paprika

1. In a large bowl, mash up all ingredients with a fork except for paprika.
2. Chill for 15 minutes, garnish with paprika, and serve on bulky white rolls with lettuce and tomato. Or just eat as is! Mmmm.

Per Serving:
Calories: 259
Fat: 14 g
Protein: 17 g

Sodium: 404 mg
Fiber: 2 g
Carbohydrates: 15 g
Sugar: 8 g

SPICY SWEET CUCUMBER SALAD

A cool and refreshing starter to get your mouth ready for the sweet and savory entrée delights to come.

SERVES 4

4 medium cucumbers, thinly sliced

1½ teaspoons salt

½ cup red wine vinegar

2 tablespoons agave nectar

2 teaspoons sesame oil

½ teaspoon crushed red pepper flakes

1 medium yellow onion, peeled and thinly sliced

1. On an ungreased baking sheet, spread out cucumbers and sprinkle with salt. Let sit for 10 minutes. Drain excess water from cucumbers.
2. Whisk together wine vinegar, agave nectar, oil, and red pepper flakes in a small bowl. Cover cucumbers with dressing and add onion slices. Toss.
3. Let sit for 10 minutes before serving.

Per Serving:
Calories: 113
Fat: 3 g
Protein: 2 g

Sodium: 300 mg
Fiber: 2 g
Carbohydrates: 22 g
Sugar: 14 g

LEMON QUINOA VEGGIE SALAD

Quinoa is great for any meal because it is so filling. You won't even need seconds. Top up the dish with a plethora of fiber-rich veggies and the spark of lemon.

SERVES 4

4 cups vegetable broth

1½ cups quinoa

1 cup frozen broccoli, thawed

¼ cup lemon juice

¼ cup olive oil

1 teaspoon garlic powder

½ teaspoon salt

¼ teaspoon ground black pepper

2 tablespoons chopped fresh Italian flat-leaf parsley

1. In a large stockpot over high heat, add vegetable broth and quinoa. Bring to a boil, and then lower heat and continue cooking on low heat, covered, for 20 minutes. Add broccoli and stir. Quinoa will be finished when all liquid has evaporated from the pan.

2. Remove from heat and add remaining ingredients. Serve. Store leftovers in the refrigerator—they'll keep for up to 5 days.

Per Serving:
Calories: 385
Fat: 18 g
Protein: 11 g

Sodium: 955 mg
Fiber: 6 g
Carbohydrates: 47 g
Sugar: 4 g

RASPBERRY VINAIGRETTE

Sweet, sharp, and perfect for a salad that is full of crisp, summery greens. Toss in some cranberries or strawberries, add some pecans or almonds, or even serve with shredded coconut and watermelon.

YIELDS 1¼ CUPS

¼ cup raspberry vinegar

2 tablespoons lime juice

¼ cup raspberry preserves

2 tablespoons Dijon mustard

½ teaspoon granulated sugar

¼ teaspoon ground nutmeg

¼ cup olive oil

⅛ teaspoon salt

⅛ teaspoon ground black pepper

1. Process all ingredients except oil, salt, and pepper in a food processor.
2. Slowly add oil, little by little, processing on high speed.
3. Season dressing with salt and pepper. Yum!

Per Serving: 2 tbsp
Calories: 92
Fat: 6 g
Protein: 0 g
Sodium: 122 mg
Fiber: 0 g
Carbohydrates: 8 g
Sugar: 6 g

CREAMY MISO SESAME DRESSING

Use this dressing on noodles or on arugula. You can also get fancy by adding some pine nuts or tangerines. The brilliant tang will wake up your mouth and may be just the push you need to get through the rest of your day.

YIELDS 1 CUP

- ¼ cup miso
- 2 tablespoons rice vinegar
- ¼ cup soy sauce
- 2 tablespoons sesame oil
- ½ cup unsweetened soy milk
- 2 tablespoons lime juice
- ½ teaspoon ground white pepper

Simply process all ingredients together in a food processor. Easy peasy!

Per Serving: 2 tbsp
Calories: 42
Fat: 3 g
Protein: 2 g
Sodium: 567 mg
Fiber: 0 g
Carbohydrates: 3 g
Sugar: 1 g

VEGAN MAYONNAISE

There are many kinds of commercial vegan mayonnaise available nowadays, but of course, the DIY kind is best. This way you know exactly what you're putting into your food, and it'll taste the freshest that it possibly can. Plus, vegan mayonnaise is low in fat and just as tasty as regular mayo. Pat yourself on the back while simultaneously spreading it on sandwiches, or use it as the base of other recipes.

YIELDS 1 CUP

1 (12-ounce) block silken tofu

1½ tablespoons lemon juice

1 teaspoon yellow mustard

1½ teaspoons apple cider vinegar

1 teaspoon granulated sugar

¾ teaspoon onion powder

½ teaspoon salt

⅓ cup canola oil

1. Process together all ingredients except oil in a food processor.
2. Add oil very slowly, one drop at a time, while processing on high speed.
3. Allow to sit covered in the refrigerator for 1 hour before serving, and voilà! Well done, master chef.

Per Serving: 1 tbsp   Sodium: 41 mg
Calories: 28   Fiber: 0 g
Fat: 3 g   Carbohydrates: 1 g
Protein: 1 g   Sugar: 0 g

PAN-ASIAN DIPPING SAUCE

If you haven't brushed up on your Pan-Asian cooking chops in the infinite spare time you have doing other things like studying physics or building an artificial heart, don't worry. This is a recipe even your least kitchen-savvy friends could figure out. Yes, including the friend who has started a small microwave fire...or two. Dip veggie sushi or edamame into this sauce, or serve it alongside tofu and steamed vegetables like broccoli and onions.

YIELDS ¼ CUP

- ¼ cup soy sauce
- 2 tablespoons rice vinegar
- 2 teaspoons sesame oil
- 1 teaspoon granulated sugar
- 1 teaspoon peeled, minced fresh ginger
- 2 cloves garlic, peeled and minced
- ¼ teaspoon crushed red pepper flakes

Simply whisk everything together in a small bowl. Done and done. Serve immediately.

Per Serving: 2 tbsp
Calories: 22
Fat: 1 g
Protein: 1 g

Sodium: 595 mg
Fiber: 0 g
Carbohydrates: 2 g
Sugar: 1 g

DAIRY-FREE RANCH DRESSING

A recipe that will have cows smiling everywhere. This is one of those things that makes you say *ah!* when you taste it. It's really remarkable when you start to discover that everything *really does* have a vegan alternative. So get your celery and carrots ready: today they shall meet their doom.

YIELDS 1 CUP

1 cup Vegan Mayonnaise (see recipe in this chapter)

¼ cup unsweetened soy milk

1 tablespoon Dijon mustard

1 tablespoon lemon juice

1 teaspoon onion powder

¾ teaspoon garlic powder

2 tablespoons chopped fresh chives

Whisk everything together in a medium bowl, adding the chives last. Store covered in the refrigerator in a closed container for up to 1 week.

Per Serving: 2 tbsp
Calories: 45
Fat: 4 g
Protein: 1 g

Sodium: 92 mg
Fiber: 0 g
Carbohydrates: 2 g
Sugar: 1 g

PAN-ASIAN RANCH DRESSING

Your favorite Pan-Asian flavors with a twist!

YIELDS ²/₃ CUP

- ½ cup Vegan Mayonnaise (see recipe in this chapter)
- ⅓ cup rice vinegar
- ¼ cup soy sauce
- 2 tablespoons sesame oil
- 2 teaspoons granulated sugar
- ½ teaspoon ground ginger
- ¾ teaspoon garlic powder
- 1 tablespoon chopped fresh chives

Mix all ingredients together in a medium bowl, adding chives in last.

Per Serving: 2 tbsp
Calories: 53
Fat: 5 g
Protein: 1 g

Sodium: 416 mg
Fiber: 0 g
Carbohydrates: 2 g
Sugar: 1 g

TO THAI FOR ORANGE PEANUT DRESSING

Mmmmmm. Say hello to your new favorite dressing. Tangy and spicy, this Indonesian peanut sauce also makes a yummy dip for veggies or a marinade for tofu.

YIELDS ¾ CUP

- ¼ cup all-natural peanut butter, room temperature
- ¼ cup no-pulp orange juice
- 2 tablespoons soy sauce
- 2 tablespoons rice vinegar
- 1 tablespoon water
- ½ teaspoon garlic powder
- ½ teaspoon granulated sugar
- ¼ teaspoon crushed red pepper flakes

Simply whisk everything together in a medium bowl, and you're ready to party. Serve immediately.

Per Serving: 2 tbsp
Calories: 67
Fat: 5 g
Protein: 3 g
Sodium: 310 mg
Fiber: 1 g
Carbohydrates: 4 g
Sugar: 2 g

OLD RELIABLE: BALSAMIC VINAIGRETTE

The old standby of salad dressings. Always there for you when the ranch or the blue cheese has gone bad. Always there for you at a neighbor's house when you dislike all of the other selections. An ode to balsamic vinaigrette. Let's hear it for him!

YIELDS 1 CUP

- ½ cup balsamic vinegar
- ¼ cup olive oil
- 1 tablespoon Dijon mustard
- ¼ teaspoon salt
- ¼ teaspoon ground black pepper
- ½ teaspoon dried basil leaves
- ½ teaspoon dried parsley leaves

Mix all ingredients together in a small bowl, blending well. Store in the refrigerator in a closed container for up to 3 days.

Per Serving: 2 tbsp
Calories: 91
Fat: 8 g
Protein: 0 g

Sodium: 146 mg
Fiber: 0 g
Carbohydrates: 3 g
Sugar: 3 g

CHAPTER 5

SOUPS

FOR THOSE LONG, COLD WINTER NIGHTS
(OR ANY TIME)

CAJUN GUMBO

If this doesn't wake up your mouth, call in the EMT. This gumbo is so rich, spicy, and fantastic that you will be dancing in your kitchen!

SERVES 5

1 medium yellow onion, peeled and diced

1 medium red bell pepper, seeded and diced

3 ribs celery, chopped

2 tablespoons olive oil

1/2 teaspoon garlic powder

1/2 teaspoon salt

1/4 teaspoon ground black pepper

1 medium zucchini, sliced

1 (14-ounce) can diced tomatoes, undrained

3 cups vegetable broth

2 teaspoons hot sauce

1 teaspoon filé powder

3/4 teaspoon dried thyme leaves

1 teaspoon Cajun seasoning

2 bay leaves

1 (15-ounce) can kidney beans, drained

1 1/2 cups cooked brown rice

1. In a large stockpot over medium-high heat, sauté onion, bell pepper, and celery for 3 minutes in oil. Toss in garlic powder, salt, and black pepper.

2. Lower the heat to medium, and add zucchini, tomatoes, and broth. Add all remaining ingredients except beans and rice. Simmer, covered, for 30 minutes.

3. Add beans, and cook for another 5 minutes to soften them up and absorb the broth. Add rice and stir. Make certain to remove the bay leaves before you eat!

Per Serving:
Calories: 247
Fat: 7 g
Protein: 9 g

Sodium: 813 mg
Fiber: 7 g
Carbohydrates: 39 g
Sugar: 9 g

CHILI FOR THOSE WHO'D RATHER NOT COOK

This hearty recipe takes only 10 minutes to make—promise. Procrastinators unite!

SERVES 4

- 1 (12-ounce) jar organic salsa
- 1 (14-ounce) can diced tomatoes, undrained
- 2 (14-ounce) cans kidney beans, drained
- 1½ cups frozen corn
- 4 frozen black bean veggie burgers, thawed and crumbled
- 2 tablespoons chili powder
- 1 teaspoon ground cumin
- ½ cup water
- ⅛ teaspoon salt
- ⅛ teaspoon ground black pepper

Combine everything in a large stockpot. Simmer over medium-high heat for about 10 minutes, and you're done. And you'll soon be full too! Thank you, fiber and protein.

Per Serving:
Calories: 328
Fat: 7 g
Protein: 16 g

Sodium: 1,508 mg
Fiber: 13 g
Carbohydrates: 57 g
Sugar: 13 g

GARLIC MISO AND ONION SOUP

An easy Asian-inspired soup with tofu to fill you up. Plain tofu can sometimes be kind of bland (sorry, tofu, but it's true). In this recipe, however, the neutral taste of tofu plays well against the miso and garlic. Hooray for an old vegan staple!

SERVES 4

5 cups water

½ cup sliced shiitake mushrooms

3 scallions, chopped

½ medium yellow onion, peeled and chopped

4 cloves garlic, peeled and minced

¾ teaspoon garlic powder

2 tablespoons soy sauce

1 teaspoon sesame oil

1 (1-pound) block silken tofu, diced

⅓ cup miso

1. Combine all ingredients except miso in a large stockpot over medium-high heat, and bring to a simmer (liquid should be moving, but no bubbles should be forming). Cook for 12 minutes.

2. Add miso. Simmer, stirring, for 5 minutes until miso is dissolved all the way through. And you're finished!

Per Serving:
Calories: 143
Fat: 6 g
Protein: 10 g

Sodium: 1,368 mg
Fiber: 2 g
Carbohydrates: 14 g
Sugar: 4 g

WINTER SEITAN STEW

A satisfying stew with big flavor. Something for those chilly evenings when you just want to make some comfort food. This dish boasts a "meaty" flavor that will recall beef stews you've had in the past.

SERVES 4

- 2 cups chopped seitan
- 1 medium yellow onion, peeled and chopped
- 2 medium carrots, peeled and chopped
- 2 ribs celery, chopped
- 2 tablespoons olive oil
- 4 cups vegetable broth
- 2 medium red potatoes, peeled and chopped
- 1/2 teaspoon dried sage
- 1/2 teaspoon dried rosemary leaves
- 1/2 teaspoon dried thyme leaves
- 2 tablespoons cornstarch
- 1/3 cup water
- 1/8 teaspoon salt
- 1/8 teaspoon ground black pepper

1. In a large stockpot over medium-high heat, cook seitan, onion, carrots, and celery in oil for 5 minutes, browning seitan a bit as you stir.
2. Add broth. Add potatoes, sage, rosemary, and thyme, and let simmer, covered, for 25 minutes.
3. Mix cornstarch and water together in a small bowl. Add mixture to the pot, stirring to mix.
4. Cook uncovered for 7 minutes, season with salt and pepper, and eat up!

Per Serving:
Calories: 373
Fat: 10 g
Protein: 28 g

Sodium: 1,322 mg
Fiber: 5 g
Carbohydrates: 44 g
Sugar: 10 g

BARLEY VEGETABLE SOUP

A great vegetable soup with a hearty, atypical grain to fill you up. The delicious broth goes well with a really crunchy baguette and some fresh pesto. It's the perfect appetizer.

SERVES 6

- 1 medium yellow onion, peeled and chopped
- 2 medium carrots, peeled and sliced
- 2 ribs celery, chopped
- 2 tablespoons olive oil
- 8 cups vegetable broth
- 1 cup barley
- 1½ cups frozen broccoli
- 1 (14-ounce) can crushed tomatoes, undrained
- ½ teaspoon chopped fresh Italian flat-leaf parsley
- ½ teaspoon dried thyme leaves
- 2 bay leaves
- ⅛ teaspoon salt
- ⅛ teaspoon ground black pepper

1. In a large stockpot over high heat, sauté onion, carrots, and celery in oil until onions are translucent, about 2 minutes.
2. Lower the heat to medium, and add remaining ingredients except salt and pepper. Simmer, covered, for 45 minutes.
3. Allow to cook uncovered for another 10 minutes. Add salt and pepper. Don't forget to remove the bay leaves before you chow down!

Per Serving:
Calories: 218
Fat: 5 g
Protein: 6 g

Sodium: 1,080 mg
Fiber: 8 g
Carbohydrates: 39 g
Sugar: 7 g

INDIAN CURRIED LENTIL SOUP

One of the perfect cuisines for vegetarians and vegans is Indian. The country with the largest number of vegetarians in the world is bound to have at least a few specialties, right? So here it is: Indian food made simple. This dish is superb with a side of warm vegan naan to dip and a silky coconut smoothie to wash it all down.

SERVES 4

1 medium yellow onion, peeled and diced

2 tablespoons vegan margarine

1 medium carrot, peeled and sliced

2 whole cloves

1 teaspoon ground turmeric

1 teaspoon ground cumin

1 cup green lentils

2¾ cups vegetable broth

2 large tomatoes, chopped

1 teaspoon salt

1 teaspoon lemon juice

¼ teaspoon ground black pepper

1. In a large stockpot over high heat, brown onion for about 3 minutes in margarine. Toss in carrot and cloves, and stir. Add turmeric and cumin, toasting for 2 minutes while stirring constantly.

2. Lower the heat to medium-low, adding all remaining ingredients except lemon juice and pepper. Simmer, covered, for 45 minutes. Check lentils to make sure they're all cooked before you remove soup from heat.

3. Remove the cloves and season soup with lemon juice and pepper. Serve.

Per Serving:
Calories: 155
Fat: 6 g
Protein: 6 g

Sodium: 1,110 mg
Fiber: 6 g
Carbohydrates: 20 g
Sugar: 6 g

CANNELLINI BEAN AND CORN CHOWDER

Never fear, chowder is here! Some folks might lament the loss of corn chowder when they become vegan, but not you, you clever devil. You've found this recipe, and there's no mourning for you. You *can* have creamy, awesome goodness as an occasional vegan.

SERVES 4

1 medium russet potato, peeled and chopped small

1 medium yellow onion, peeled and chopped

2 tablespoons olive oil

3 cups vegetable broth

1 tablespoon whole-wheat flour

1½ cups unsweetened soy milk

1 (16-ounce) bag frozen corn

1 (14-ounce) can cannellini beans, drained

½ teaspoon dried thyme leaves

¼ teaspoon ground black pepper

1. In a large stockpot over high heat, sauté potato and onion in oil for 5 minutes.
2. Turn the heat down to medium-low, and add broth, letting cook, covered, for another 20 minutes.
3. In a medium bowl, whisk flour and milk together until smooth. Add to the pot.
4. Add corn, beans, thyme, and pepper to the pot. Reduce heat to low and cook for 5 minutes, stirring frequently. Chow down on this chow-der!

Per Serving:
Calories: 347
Fat: 10 g
Protein: 13 g

Sodium: 689 mg
Fiber: 8 g
Carbohydrates: 56 g
Sugar: 12 g

SPICY ROASTED TOMATO SOUP

This warm and zesty soup is perfect for a fall day. Combining the natural sweetness of tomatoes with the spice of cayenne, it is a tasty pick-me-up. The key to this recipe is finding the freshest ingredients you can. The tastes will be bright and soothing. Just don't get too excited now—you haven't even started cooking yet!

SERVES 4

6 large tomatoes, chopped

1 small yellow onion, peeled and chopped

4 cloves garlic, peeled

2 tablespoons olive oil

1 teaspoon cayenne pepper

1/4 teaspoon ground black pepper

1/4 teaspoon ground cumin

3/4 teaspoon salt

1/8 teaspoon ground nutmeg

1 1/4 cups unsweetened soy milk

2 tablespoons chopped fresh basil

1 1/2 teaspoons balsamic vinegar

1/2 teaspoon red wine

1. Preheat oven to 450°F.
2. Spread tomatoes and onion on an ungreased baking sheet alongside garlic. Drizzle with oil and sprinkle with both peppers, cumin, salt, and nutmeg. Bake for 1 hour.
3. Blend seasoned tomatoes and all remaining ingredients together in a food processor.
4. Transfer to a medium saucepan and cook over high heat for 2 minutes.

Per Serving:
Calories: 171
Fat: 9 g
Protein: 6 g

Sodium: 491 mg
Fiber: 4 g
Carbohydrates: 20 g
Sugar: 12 g

WHITE BEAN AND ORZO MINESTRONE

A delicious Italian staple that even your Nonna will be impressed by. *Perfetto!*

SERVES 6

3 cloves garlic, peeled and minced

1 medium yellow onion, peeled and chopped

2 ribs celery, chopped

2 tablespoons olive oil

5 cups vegetable broth

1 medium carrot, peeled and diced

1 cup chopped fresh green beans

2 small red potatoes, peeled and chopped small

2 medium tomatoes, chopped

1 (15-ounce) can cannellini beans, drained

1 teaspoon dried basil leaves

1/2 teaspoon dried oregano leaves

1/4 cup orzo

1/8 teaspoon salt

1/8 teaspoon ground black pepper

1. Over medium-high heat, combine garlic, onion, and celery with oil in a large stockpot. Cook for about 3 minutes, stirring frequently.

2. Add in broth, carrot, green beans, potatoes, tomatoes, beans, basil, and oregano. Bring to a simmer over medium heat (liquid should be moving, but no bubbles should be forming). Cover and cook for 25 minutes.

3. Add orzo and cook for another 10 minutes. Season with salt and pepper.

Per Serving:
Calories: 211
Fat: 6 g
Protein: 7 g

Sodium: 726 mg
Fiber: 6 g
Carbohydrates: 35 g
Sugar: 7 g

NOT-CHICKEN SOUP

Just as comforting and soulful as the real thing. When you've got the sniffles, whip up a pot of this soup. Then shuffle back to your bed, encase yourself in your comfiest comforter, put on a terrible TV show, and eat yourself back to health.

SERVES 6

- 6 cups vegetable broth
- 1 medium carrot, peeled and diced
- 2 ribs celery, diced
- 1 medium yellow onion, peeled and chopped
- 1 "chicken"-flavored vegan bouillon cube
- 2 bay leaves
- 1½ teaspoons Italian seasoning
- ⅛ teaspoon salt
- ⅛ teaspoon ground black pepper
- 1 tablespoon nutritional yeast
- 1 cup cooked brown rice
- 2 teaspoons chili powder

Simply combine all ingredients in a large pot and let simmer over low heat for 30 minutes. Easy!

THE SKINNY ON...VEGAN-STYLE MEAT FLAVORINGS

Sometimes you get tired of veggie broth and want to mix it up. Believe it or not, there are many brands of "beef"- or "chicken"-flavored vegan bouillon cubes. These faux-meat flavorings can be found in natural food stores and are usually composed of a compressed mixture of yeasts, palm oil, herbs, dried veggies, and spices.

Per Serving:
Calories: 74
Fat: 1 g
Protein: 2 g

Sodium: 755 mg
Fiber: 2 g
Carbohydrates: 15 g
Sugar: 3 g

SHIITAKE AND GARLIC BROTH

Do you ever try something once and then love it so much that you go back and eat it every night for a month? This is one of those dishes. There's no getting out of it. We're in deep shiitake, friends.

YIELDS 6 CUPS

- ⅓ cup dried shiitake mushrooms
- 6 cups water
- 2 cloves garlic, peeled and smashed
- 1 bay leaf
- ½ teaspoon dried thyme leaves
- ½ medium yellow onion, peeled and chopped

1. Combine all ingredients in a large pot, and bring to a simmer over low heat (liquid should be moving, but no bubbles should be forming). Cook for about 40 minutes.
2. Strain out the vegetables before using the stock in another soup.

Per Serving: 1 cup
Calories: 29
Fat: 0 g
Protein: 1 g

Sodium: 2 mg
Fiber: 1 g
Carbohydrates: 7 g
Sugar: 1 g

POTATO AND LEEK SOUP

Just want to curl up in a homey mansion nestled somewhere in the country estates of Surrey? Well, you probably can't, but you can make this classic English comfort soup. In all senses of the word, this soup will root you warmly into a pleasant, restful mood.

SERVES 6

1 medium yellow onion, peeled and diced

2 cloves garlic, peeled and minced

2 tablespoons olive oil

6 cups vegetable broth

3 leeks, sliced

2 large red potatoes, peeled and sliced

2 bay leaves

1 cup unsweetened soy milk

2 tablespoons vegan margarine

¾ teaspoon salt

⅓ teaspoon ground black pepper

½ teaspoon dried sage

½ teaspoon dried thyme leaves

2 tablespoons nutritional yeast

1. In a large stockpot over high heat, sauté onion and garlic in oil for about 2 minutes.
2. Add broth, leeks, potatoes, and bay leaves. Bring the heat down to medium, and cook for about 30 minutes until potatoes are done.
3. Remove bay leaves. Purée mixture in a food processor, then return to the pot and add remaining ingredients. Cook for another 3 minutes over medium-high heat.

Per Serving:
Calories: 233
Fat: 9 g
Protein: 6 g

Sodium: 1,038 mg
Fiber: 5 g
Carbohydrates: 33 g
Sugar: 7 g

CASHEW CREAM OF ASPARAGUS SOUP

Filling, tasty, and hearty, this low-calorie soup packs 10 grams of protein thanks to the delicious cashew nuts. This unexpected combination melds wonderfully for a hot soup perfect for dipping warm pieces of garlic bread. You'll certainly have something to be thankful for this faux Thanksgiving.

SERVES 4

- 1 medium yellow onion, peeled and chopped
- 4 cloves garlic, peeled and minced
- 2 tablespoons olive oil
- 2 pounds fresh asparagus, trimmed and chopped
- 4 cups vegetable broth
- ¾ cup raw cashews
- ¾ cup water
- ¼ teaspoon dried sage
- ½ teaspoon salt
- ¼ teaspoon ground black pepper
- 2 teaspoons lemon juice
- 2 tablespoons nutritional yeast

1. In a large pot over medium-high heat, sauté onion and garlic in oil for about 3 minutes. Add asparagus and broth. Bring to a simmer (liquid should be moving, but no bubbles should be forming), and cover. Cook for 20 minutes.

2. Transfer mixture to a food processor. Process until nearly smooth and put back in the pot.

3. Purée cashews and water in the food processor. Add mixture to the pot. Add in remaining ingredients. Serve with garlic bread.

Per Serving:
Calories: 177
Fat: 12 g
Protein: 10 g

Sodium: 954 mg
Fiber: 4 g
Carbohydrates: 14 g
Sugar: 5 g

VEGETARIAN "BEEF" AND BARLEY STEW

Steak, burgers...beef can make it so hard to be vegan. This recipe has a delicious beefy flavor that will satisfy your cravings—meat-free!

SERVES 4

- 1 medium yellow onion, peeled and chopped
- 2 ribs celery, chopped
- 1 medium carrot, peeled and chopped
- 1 medium green bell pepper, seeded and chopped
- 2 tablespoons olive oil
- 1 cup water
- 1/2 cup tomato juice
- 1/3 cup barley
- 1 1/2 teaspoons chili powder
- 1 1/2 teaspoons chopped fresh Italian flat-leaf parsley
- 2 bay leaves
- 3 frozen veggie burgers, thawed and crumbled
- 1/8 teaspoon salt
- 1/8 teaspoon ground black pepper

1. In a large stockpot over medium-high heat, cook onion, celery, carrot, and bell pepper in oil for 4 minutes to soften.
2. Add water, tomato juice, and barley to the pot. Stir, then add chili powder, parsley, and bay leaves. Stir. Cover and cook for 20 minutes.
3. Add veggie burgers and cook for another 5 minutes. Season with salt and black pepper, and remember to remove the bay leaves before eating!

Per Serving:
Calories: 221
Fat: 9 g
Protein: 5 g

Sodium: 507 mg
Fiber: 9 g
Carbohydrates: 34 g
Sugar: 5 g

BARLEY AND BELL PEPPER CHILI

This chili is hearty and satisfying thanks to crunchy whole grains used in place of beef. The bell pepper and dash of nutmeg give a sweet touch to this traditionally spicy chili dish. Sweet and spicy? A perfect date.

SERVES 6

- 3 cloves garlic, peeled and minced
- 1 medium yellow onion, peeled and chopped
- 2 medium red bell peppers, seeded and chopped
- 2 tablespoons olive oil
- 1/2 cup barley
- 1/2 cup vegetable broth
- 1 (15-ounce) can diced tomatoes, undrained
- 1 (15-ounce) can black beans, drained
- 2 tablespoons chili powder
- 1 teaspoon ground cumin
- 1/2 teaspoon dried oregano leaves
- 1/2 teaspoon ground nutmeg
- 2 tablespoons chopped fresh cilantro

1. In a large stockpot over medium-high heat, sauté garlic, onion, and bell peppers in oil for 3 minutes. Add barley and toast for 1 minute until it becomes brownish in color.

2. Reduce heat to low, and add broth, tomatoes, beans, chili powder, cumin, oregano, and nutmeg. Bring to a simmer (liquid should be moving, but no bubbles should be forming), cover, and cook for 35 minutes. Top with cilantro before serving.

Per Serving:
Calories: 198
Fat: 6 g
Protein: 7 g

Sodium: 456 mg
Fiber: 10 g
Carbohydrates: 33 g
Sugar: 6 g

CHAPTER 6

EASY SIDES

FOR THE MOTIVATIONALLY DISINCLINED

ROASTED GARLIC MASHED TATERS

There is nothing in the world more comforting than mashed potatoes. Leave the skin on the potatoes—that's where all the nutrients live. The garlic and olive oil in this recipe will keep everything moist, while the soy cream and nutritional yeast will ensure the creamy flavor that you crave.

SERVES 4

1 head garlic, outer shell removed

2 tablespoons olive oil

6 medium red potatoes, cooked

½ cup vegan margarine

½ cup soy cream

2 teaspoons dried rosemary leaves

2 tablespoons nutritional yeast

⅛ teaspoon salt

⅛ teaspoon ground black pepper

1. Preheat oven to 400°F.
2. Drizzle garlic generously with oil on an ungreased baking sheet and cover with aluminum foil. Bake for about 30 minutes.
3. In a large bowl, press garlic cloves out of their skins and mash them up with a fork.
4. Combine all remaining ingredients in the bowl, and season with salt and pepper, mashing potatoes to desired consistency. Voilà!

Per Serving:
Calories: 523
Fat: 30 g
Protein: 8 g

Sodium: 403 mg
Fiber: 6 g
Carbohydrates: 58 g
Sugar: 7 g

GINGERED AND PRALINED SWEET POTATOES

Candied sweetness for your favorite holidays. There are also vegan marshmallows available in some chain food stores for a sweeter touch. Top with a little bit of **vegan brown sugar** and you're all set.

SERVES 4

4 medium sweet potatoes, peeled and baked

¼ cup soy cream

¼ cup no-pulp orange juice

½ teaspoon salt

½ cup chopped pecans

2 tablespoons vegan margarine

⅓ cup maple syrup

½ cup whole-wheat flour

½ cup candied ginger

½ cup rolled oats

1 tablespoon light brown sugar

1. Preheat oven to 350°F.
2. Mash together sweet potatoes, cream, orange juice, and salt in a large bowl. Transfer mixture to a greased 9" × 13" casserole dish.
3. Combine remaining ingredients in a small bowl and then spread on top of sweet potato mixture.
4. Bake for 30 minutes, and you're done, done, done.

Per Serving:
Calories: 538
Fat: 19 g
Protein: 7 g

Sodium: 437 mg
Fiber: 9 g
Carbohydrates: 88 g
Sugar: 41 g

SESAME SOY ASPARAGUS AND MUSHROOMS

The flavor of sesame is nutty and sweet, and mushrooms lend this dish an earthy flavor that is picked up by the bright notes in the asparagus. This recipe makes a great side to any meal. And it can be colorful too: asparagus comes in white, green, and even purple!

SERVES 4

1 pound fresh asparagus, trimmed and chopped

¾ cup chopped white mushrooms

2 teaspoons sesame oil

1 teaspoon soy sauce

½ teaspoon granulated sugar

½ teaspoon ground white pepper

2 tablespoons sesame seeds

1. Preheat oven to 350°F.
2. Place asparagus and mushrooms in an ungreased 9" × 13" baking dish. Roast for about 10 minutes.
3. Remove from the oven, and drizzle with oil and soy sauce. Then sprinkle with sugar and pepper. Toss. Return to the oven for about 6 minutes.
4. Toss vegetables with sesame seeds and serve.

THE SKINNY ON...SUGAR

Many sugars are bleached using bone char—this includes brown sugars too! Brown sugars are commonly flavored with molasses, which is what provides the distinctive tang. To make certain your sugar is vegan, check with the manufacturer.

Per Serving:
Calories: 64
Fat: 5 g
Protein: 3 g

Sodium: 86 mg
Fiber: 2 g
Carbohydrates: 5 g
Sugar: 2 g

CRANBERRY APPLE STUFFING

Missing autumn? The pumpkins? The cornstalks? The apple pies loaded with goodness and ice cream? This stuffing will satisfy all those urges and hearken back to those spicy cinnamon and clove aromas that you fall in love with every time the leaves change. Enjoy this with some hot mulled cider.

SERVES 6

- 2 tablespoons vegan margarine
- 1 medium yellow onion, peeled and diced
- ⅔ cup white mushrooms, chopped
- ¾ teaspoon dried sage
- ¾ teaspoon dried thyme leaves
- ½ teaspoon dried marjoram
- 12 slices whole-wheat bread, cubed
- 1 cup dried cranberries
- 1 large red apple, peeled and diced
- ½ cup apple juice
- 2 cups vegetable broth
- ⅛ teaspoon salt
- ⅛ teaspoon ground black pepper

1. Preheat oven to 350°F.
2. In a large saucepan on low heat, melt margarine for 30 seconds. Add onion and mushrooms, letting them cook about 4 minutes until soft. Add sage, thyme, and marjoram, and heat for another 2 minutes.
3. Stir in remaining ingredients, mixing thoroughly. Place in a greased 9" × 13" casserole dish and bake for 30 minutes.

Per Serving:
Calories: 299
Fat: 6 g
Protein: 8 g

Sodium: 565 mg
Fiber: 6 g
Carbohydrates: 56 g
Sugar: 29 g

GARLIC AND SOY SAUCE GREEN BEANS

Remember: fresh green beans are always better than frozen or canned (blah). They're pretty cheap too, so pick some up the next time you're out. They have a crunch that is simply something else when they're left a little al dente.

SERVES 4

1 pound fresh green beans, trimmed and chopped

2 tablespoons olive oil

1/2 teaspoon crushed red pepper flakes

4 cloves garlic, peeled and minced

1 teaspoon peeled, minced fresh ginger

3 tablespoons soy sauce

1/8 teaspoon ground black pepper

1. Add green beans to a large pot and cover with water. Cover and boil over high heat for about 3 minutes. Drain and set aside.
2. Heat oil in a large skillet, and toss in red pepper flakes, garlic, ginger, and cooked green beans. Cook for about 3 minutes.
3. Season with soy sauce and black pepper. Yum!

Per Serving:
Calories: 104
Fat: 7 g
Protein: 3 g

Sodium: 761 mg
Fiber: 3 g
Carbohydrates: 9 g
Sugar: 4 g

SAUCY INDIAN VEGGIES

Indian chefs are seriously talented. Here is our ode to their finesse. This rich-tasting veggie dish also just happens to be low in calories.

SERVES 4

1 (28-ounce) can diced tomatoes, undrained

2 medium red potatoes, peeled and chopped

½ teaspoon chili powder

2 teaspoons curry powder

1½ teaspoons ground cumin

½ teaspoon ground turmeric

1 medium head cauliflower, chopped

1 medium carrot, peeled and diced

¾ cup frozen green peas

¾ teaspoon crushed red pepper flakes

¼ teaspoon salt

1. Mix tomatoes, potatoes, chili powder, curry powder, cumin, and turmeric in a large pot and cover. Cook for 10 minutes over medium heat.

2. Add remaining ingredients and cook for another 15 minutes. Use a fork to make sure potatoes are soft before removing from heat.

Per Serving:
Calories: 210
Fat: 2 g
Protein: 10 g

Sodium: 617 mg
Fiber: 11 g
Carbohydrates: 45 g
Sugar: 15 g

SWEETENED ROAST SQUASH

Delicious and autumnal. Reach for this dish in the fall when squash is in season and there is a nip in the air that calls for a hearty, spicy side that'll warm you from your nose to your toes.

SERVES 4

1 large butternut squash, peeled, quartered, and seeded

1 teaspoon sea salt

4 tablespoons no-pulp orange juice

4 tablespoons maple syrup

$\frac{1}{6}$ teaspoon ground nutmeg

$\frac{1}{6}$ teaspoon ground cinnamon

1. Preheat oven to 400°F.
2. Place squash in a greased 9" × 13" casserole dish. Sprinkle each quarter with an equal amount of salt, orange juice, syrup, nutmeg, and cinnamon.
3. Cover with foil and bake for 45 minutes. Enjoy the scent of fall!

Per Serving:
Calories: 151
Fat: 0 g
Protein: 2 g

Sodium: 593 mg
Fiber: 7 g
Carbohydrates: 39 g
Sugar: 18 g

BAKED SWEET POTATO FRIES

Waaaaaaaaaaay better than french fries. Don't even go there. Sweet, crunchy, and so much tastier. These puppies go great with a side of honey and a sprinkling of cinnamon and sugar. Or just be old school and eat them with a dash of salt and ketchup. Make them spicy by adding some Cajun seasoning, nutritional yeast, or a little cayenne pepper, or eat them dipped in a vegan cheese dip.

SERVES 2

2 large sweet potatoes, peeled and sliced thin into fries

2 tablespoons olive oil

¼ teaspoon garlic powder

½ teaspoon paprika

½ teaspoon light brown sugar

½ teaspoon chili powder

½ teaspoon salt

1. Preheat oven to 400°F.
2. Spread out fries on an ungreased baking sheet and brush with oil on all sides.
3. In a small bowl, combine all spices and sprinkle over fries.
4. Cook for 10 minutes, turning once after 5 minutes. Eat up!

Per Serving:
Calories: 240
Fat: 14 g
Protein: 2 g

Sodium: 673 mg
Fiber: 4 g
Carbohydrates: 28 g
Sugar: 7 g

HONEY MUSTARD AND BALSAMIC VINEGAR GREEN BEANS

Green beans are crunchy, satisfying, and delicious. Enjoy this tangy, satisfying dish as a healthy lunch!

SERVES 1

¼ medium red onion, peeled and chopped

½ medium white onion, peeled and chopped

3 cloves garlic, peeled and minced

1 tablespoon olive oil

½ pound cooked fresh green beans

½ cup fresh broccoli florets

½ teaspoon paprika

⅛ teaspoon salt

⅛ teaspoon ground black pepper

1½ tablespoons honey mustard

⅛ cup balsamic vinegar

1 tablespoon nutritional yeast

1. In a large pan over medium-high heat, sauté onions and garlic in oil for about 3 minutes, stirring constantly. Add green beans and broccoli, and stir to coat in olive oil.

2. Continue cooking for 1 minute, then add paprika, salt, and pepper. Stir. Add honey mustard and vinegar. Continue stirring and cook for 1 minute.

3. Sprinkle with nutritional yeast and serve warm.

Per Serving:
Calories: 325
Fat: 15 g
Protein: 10 g

Sodium: 491 mg
Fiber: 11 g
Carbohydrates: 42 g
Sugar: 21 g

CARAMELIZED BABY CARROTS

Sweet and small—itty-bitty and just so cute you'll want to devour them the second they're finished. Watch. You will.

SERVES 4

- 4 cups baby carrots
- 1 teaspoon lemon juice
- 2 tablespoons vegan margarine
- 1 tablespoon maple syrup
- 2 tablespoons light brown sugar
- 1/2 teaspoon sea salt

1. In a large saucepan over medium-low heat, simmer carrots in water for about 8 minutes until soft and cooked through. Drain, and drizzle with lemon juice.

2. Turn heat to medium-high, and add margarine, syrup, brown sugar, and salt to pan. Cook carrots for another 5 minutes until they glaze over, and you should be golden! Er... caramelized!

Per Serving:
Calories: 110
Fat: 6 g
Protein: 0 g

Sodium: 400 mg
Fiber: 2 g
Carbohydrates: 15 g
Sugar: 13 g

SWEET STUFFED BUTTERNUT SQUASH

Some people love sweet potatoes, but butternut squash is here to steal your heart (and stomach). It manages to be sweet and soft without getting mushy, as potatoes sometimes become. Yet another easy and nutritional recipe to add to your already stellar repertoire!

SERVES 4

- ½ cup apple juice
- 2 small butternut squash, peeled, sliced lengthwise, and seeded
- 2 medium red apples, peeled and diced
- ½ cup chopped pecans
- ⅓ cup dried cranberries
- ¼ cup maple syrup
- 2 tablespoons vegan margarine, melted
- ½ teaspoon ground cinnamon
- ¼ teaspoon ground nutmeg

1. Preheat oven to 350°F.
2. Pour apple juice into a nonstick baking sheet with a lip, and place squash on the sheet cut side up. Roast for 20 minutes.
3. In a large bowl, mix apples, pecans, and cranberries. Add syrup, margarine, cinnamon, and nutmeg. Stir well.
4. Stuff squash with filling, and roast for another 25 minutes.

Per Serving:
Calories: 402
Fat: 16 g
Protein: 4 g

Sodium: 74 mg
Fiber: 9 g
Carbohydrates: 69 g
Sugar: 40 g

CLASSIC GREEN BEAN CASSEROLE

Everyone likes a little veggies with their fried onions. Wait—shouldn't that be the other way around? Well, nobody will be asking questions when the dish tastes this good.

SERVES 4

1 (12-ounce) bag frozen green beans

¾ cup sliced white mushrooms

2 tablespoons vegan margarine

2 tablespoons white whole-wheat flour

1½ cups unsweetened soy milk

1 tablespoon Dijon mustard

½ teaspoon garlic powder

½ teaspoon salt

¼ teaspoon chopped fresh Italian flat-leaf parsley

⅓ teaspoon dried oregano leaves

¼ teaspoon ground black pepper

1½ cups french-fried onions

1. Preheat oven to 375°F. Place green beans and mushrooms in a greased 9" × 13" casserole dish.

2. In a small saucepan over low heat, melt margarine for 30 seconds and add in flour until a paste forms. Add milk, mustard, garlic powder, salt, parsley, oregano, and pepper. Stir.

3. Pour sauce over mushrooms and green beans, and top with french-fried onions. Bake for 18 minutes until onions are toasted.

Per Serving:
Calories: 274
Fat: 18 g
Protein: 5 g

Sodium: 669 mg
Fiber: 3 g
Carbohydrates: 23 g
Sugar: 5 g

EASY FALAFEL PATTIES

Falafel is both scrumptious and filling. Make mouthwatering sandwiches with falafel patties, lettuce, tomato, a little hummus, and tahini.

SERVES 4

1 (15-ounce) can chickpeas, drained

1 tablespoon white whole-wheat flour

1 teaspoon ground cumin

3/4 teaspoon garlic powder

1/2 medium yellow onion, peeled and minced

3/4 teaspoon salt

1/4 teaspoon paprika

Egg replacement mixture (equivalent of 1 egg), prepared according to package directions

1/4 cup chopped fresh Italian flat-leaf parsley

2 tablespoons chopped fresh cilantro

1. Preheat oven to 375°F.
2. Pulse chickpeas in a food processor until finely chopped.
3. Add flour, cumin, garlic powder, onion, salt, paprika, and egg replacer to the processor. Pulse. Add parsley and cilantro, and pulse until blended.
4. Shape batter into 4 patties and bake for 15 minutes on a baking sheet greased with vegan margarine, turning over once halfway through cooking.

Per Serving:
Calories: 115
Fat: 2 g
Protein: 6 g

Sodium: 602 mg
Fiber: 5 g
Carbohydrates: 19 g
Sugar: 4 g

FIVE-MINUTE VEGAN PASTA SALAD

Easy to make, easier to eat. Even the description is short! Just check the dressing label to make sure it's vegan.

SERVES 4

4 cups cooked pasta

1/4 cup vegan Italian salad dressing

3 scallions, chopped

1/2 cup sliced black olives

1/2 cup roasted red peppers

1 (14-ounce) can chickpeas, drained and rinsed

1 medium tomato, chopped

1 medium avocado, peeled, pitted, and diced

1/8 teaspoon salt

1/8 teaspoon ground black pepper

Simply toss together all ingredients. Store covered in the refrigerator for 1 hour before serving.

Per Serving:
Calories: 465
Fat: 16 g
Protein: 14 g

Sodium: 582 mg
Fiber: 11 g
Carbohydrates: 68 g
Sugar: 7 g

BLACK QUINOA WITH LIME AND RICE VINEGAR

In the mood for something with a bit of heat and tang? In the mood for something that will take about 20 minutes to prepare because you're lazy like us? Look no further! This succulent side dish works just as well as a main course.

SERVES 4

1 cup black quinoa

1½ cups water

½ tablespoon canola oil

1 medium red bell pepper, seeded and chopped

¾ medium yellow onion, peeled and chopped

¼ teaspoon salt

½ teaspoon ground white pepper

2 tablespoons lime juice

1 teaspoon cayenne pepper

3 teaspoons rice vinegar

¼ teaspoon paprika

1. In a large saucepan over high heat, mix quinoa and water. Bring to a boil, and then reduce heat to low. Simmer, covered, for approximately 20 minutes.

2. While quinoa simmers, heat oil over medium-high heat in a different large saucepan. Add bell pepper and cook for 5 minutes, then add onion and cook for another 3 minutes.

3. Remove quinoa from heat, and add peppers and onions. Add remaining ingredients, stir, and serve.

THE SKINNY ON...FRYING OILS

Canola, sesame, and coconut oils are the best oils to fry in. This is because their chemical composition resists change at the high temperatures used during frying! Hooray for science, right? Also, the lack of flavor in canola oil and coconut oil helps keep the flavor of the frying ingredients unspoiled.

Per Serving:
Calories: 192
Fat: 5 g
Protein: 7 g

Sodium: 150 mg
Fiber: 4 g
Carbohydrates: 32 g
Sugar: 3 g

EASY GARLIC QUINOA

You can never have too much garlic: it has both antiviral and antibacterial properties! This is an easy dish to mix with some veggies, if you so wish.

SERVES 4

1 medium yellow onion, peeled and diced

4 cloves garlic, peeled and minced

2 tablespoons vegan margarine

3 cups vegetable broth

1½ cups quinoa

½ teaspoon salt

½ teaspoon ground black pepper

2 tablespoons nutritional yeast

1. In a large stockpot over medium-high heat, sauté onion and garlic in margarine for about 3 minutes. Add broth and quinoa, cover, and let simmer for 15 minutes.
2. Fluff up quinoa with a fork when cooked, and stir in salt, pepper, and nutritional yeast.

Per Serving:
Calories: 316
Fat: 10 g
Protein: 11 g

Sodium: 849 mg
Fiber: 5 g
Carbohydrates: 47 g
Sugar: 4 g

LEMON CILANTRO COUSCOUS

A cheery side dish that is far from heavy. Couscous is the cutest word ever, and it is also a whole-wheat semolina pasta, rather than a whole grain like some may think. Eat this dish with some sautéed spinach or roasted squash, eggplant, and red onions.

SERVES 4

2 cups vegetable broth

1 cup couscous

1/3 cup lemon juice

1/2 cup chopped fresh cilantro

1/4 teaspoon sea salt

1. In a large saucepan over medium-high heat, bring broth to a simmer (liquid should be moving, but no bubbles should be forming). Add couscous and cover. Cook for 10 minutes.
2. Add lemon juice, cilantro, and salt. Enjoy!

Per Serving:
Calories: 173
Fat: 0 g
Protein: 6 g

Sodium: 478 mg
Fiber: 2 g
Carbohydrates: 36 g
Sugar: 1 g

BARLEY PILAF WITH EDAMAME AND ROASTED RED PEPPER

This atypical pilaf recipe brings in a ton of unexpected flavors plus added protein from the edamame. This dish also tastes great both warm and cold!

SERVES 6

2 cups frozen shelled edamame, thawed and drained

2 cups cooked barley

½ cup roasted red peppers

⅔ cup frozen green peas, thawed

⅔ cup frozen corn, thawed

1½ tablespoons Dijon mustard

2 tablespoons lemon juice

¾ teaspoon garlic powder

2 tablespoons olive oil

⅛ teaspoon salt

⅛ teaspoon ground black pepper

½ cup chopped fresh cilantro

1 medium avocado, peeled, pitted, and diced

1. Mix edamame, barley, red peppers, peas, and corn in a large bowl. Give them a good toss.

2. In a small bowl, whisk together mustard, lemon juice, garlic powder, and oil. Pour over barley mixture.

3. Season with salt, black pepper, and cilantro. Toss and then top with avocado.

Per Serving:
Calories: 243
Fat: 12 g
Protein: 9 g

Sodium: 209 mg
Fiber: 8 g
Carbohydrates: 26 g
Sugar: 3 g

SPICED COUSCOUS SALAD WITH BELL PEPPER AND ZUCCHINI

This dish is a combination of Middle Eastern spices and vegetables. A perfect side dish or meal itself—just pair with some toasted whole-grain pita bread and crunch away.

SERVES 4

- 2 cups vegetable broth
- 2 cups couscous
- 1 teaspoon ground cumin
- ½ teaspoon ground turmeric
- ½ teaspoon paprika
- ¼ teaspoon cayenne pepper
- 1 tablespoon lemon juice
- 2 medium zucchini, sliced
- 1 medium red bell pepper, seeded and chopped
- 1 medium yellow bell pepper, seeded and chopped
- 3 cloves garlic, peeled and minced
- ½ medium white onion, peeled and chopped
- 2 tablespoons olive oil
- 2 tablespoons chopped fresh Italian flat-leaf parsley
- ⅛ teaspoon salt
- ⅛ teaspoon ground black pepper

1. In a large stockpot over medium heat, mix together broth and couscous, and bring broth to a boil. Add cumin, turmeric, paprika, and cayenne pepper, and stir.

2. Shut the heat off and cover the pot, leaving couscous to sit for 15 minutes. Broth should be fully absorbed when the time is up. Add lemon juice and mix, mix, mix.

3. In a medium saucepan over medium-high heat, sauté zucchini, bell peppers, garlic, and onion in oil, about 5 minutes. Mix into the couscous.

4. Add parsley, salt, and black pepper. Give yourself a pat on the back.

Per Serving:
Calories: 440
Fat: 8 g
Protein: 14 g

Sodium: 422 mg
Fiber: 7 g
Carbohydrates: 78 g
Sugar: 6 g

FRUITY FALL QUINOA

If you want to keep this sweet, simply omit the parsley, thyme, celery, and onion. That way you can eat it warm for breakfast on a cool day. You can sweeten quinoa dishes even more by subbing almond or soy milk for water.

SERVES 4

- 1 cup red or white quinoa
- 2 cups apple juice
- 1 cup water
- 2 tablespoons vegan margarine
- 1/2 medium yellow onion, peeled and diced
- 2 ribs celery, diced
- 1/2 teaspoon ground nutmeg
- 1/2 teaspoon ground cinnamon
- 1/4 teaspoon ground cloves
- 1/2 cup dried cranberries
- 1/2 cup chopped dried apricots
- 1 teaspoon dried thyme leaves
- 1 teaspoon chopped fresh Italian flat-leaf parsley
- 1/4 teaspoon salt

1. In a large stockpot, combine quinoa with apple juice and water. Bring to a boil over medium-high heat, then let simmer on low heat for 15 minutes.
2. In a medium saucepan over medium-high heat, melt margarine for 30 seconds, then sauté onion and celery for about 3 minutes until soft. Add to quinoa mixture and stir for 1 minute.
3. Toss in remaining ingredients, and cook over low heat for 4 minutes, just to warm it up and let all the flavors mingle.

PART-TIME TIP

Stir-frying is quite possibly the easiest and quickest way to whip up a meal. Since stir-frying requires you to cook at high temperatures, try to keep an arm's length away from your wok to avoid painful oil burns.

Per Serving:
Calories: 376
Fat: 9 g
Protein: 7 g

Sodium: 232 mg
Fiber: 7 g
Carbohydrates: 71 g
Sugar: 37 g

COUSCOUS AND BEAN PILAF

We've been tossing beans, pilafs, and couscous around here for a while. We might as well combine them! The real invention in cooking comes when you have only certain ingredients left in the house. You ask yourself, *What the heck am I going to make?* And then voilà: your masterpiece somehow comes to life using veggie broth, beans, and parsley.

SERVES 4

2 cups vegetable broth

2 cups couscous

2 tablespoons olive oil

2 tablespoons red wine vinegar

1/2 teaspoon crushed red pepper flakes

2 tablespoons minced pimento peppers

1 tablespoon chopped fresh Italian flat-leaf parsley

1 (15-ounce) can cannellini beans, drained

1/8 teaspoon salt

1/8 teaspoon ground black pepper

1. In a large stockpot over medium-low heat, bring broth to a simmer (liquid should be moving, but no bubbles should be forming). Then drop couscous in. Cover and let cook for 15 minutes.

2. In a small bowl, mix oil and vinegar. It's best if you use a whisk to do this. Add red pepper flakes. Pour over couscous.

3. Fluff in the pimento peppers, parsley, and beans. Season with salt and pepper.

Per Serving:
Calories: 474
Fat: 8 g
Protein: 17 g

Sodium: 558 mg
Fiber: 8 g
Carbohydrates: 82 g
Sugar: 4 g

BARLEY BAKED BEANS

Rich but not heavy, this dish has the sweet molasses flavor of traditional baked beans. This is a side that would go perfectly with roasted corn and vegan ribs (many varieties of vegan barbecue are available in the frozen foods section of your grocery store). So kick back with a cold beer, and try this dish at your next barbecue.

SERVES 8

2 cups cooked barley

2 (15-ounce) cans pinto beans, drained

1 medium yellow onion, peeled and diced

1 (28-ounce) can crushed tomatoes, undrained

½ cup water

¼ cup light brown sugar

⅓ cup barbecue sauce

2 tablespoons molasses

2 teaspoons mustard powder

1 teaspoon garlic powder

1 teaspoon salt

1. Preheat oven to 300°F.
2. Combine all ingredients in an ungreased 9" × 13" casserole dish, cover, and bake for 2 hours.
3. Uncover and cook for another 15 minutes. Finger lickin' good, chef!

Per Serving:
Calories: 187
Fat: 1 g
Protein: 5 g

Sodium: 402 mg
Fiber: 4 g
Carbohydrates: 42 g
Sugar: 20 g

AGAVE MUSTARD-GLAZED TOFU

A sweet and zesty dish perfect with some Barley Baked Beans (see recipe in this chapter) or at a barbecue with vegan dogs and veggie burgers.

SERVES 3

1 (1-pound) block extra-firm tofu, chopped into cubes

2 tablespoons lemon juice

2 tablespoons water

1 teaspoon soy sauce

1/4 cup agave nectar

2 tablespoons yellow mustard

1/2 teaspoon garlic powder

1/2 teaspoon granulated sugar

3/4 teaspoon curry powder

1. Place tofu in an ungreased 9" × 13" casserole dish. In a small bowl, whisk up all remaining ingredients, then pour over tofu. Let marinate for 1 hour, stirring occasionally so that tofu is evenly covered.
2. Preheat oven to 400°F.
3. Bake for 25 minutes, then relax and enjoy.

Per Serving:
Calories: 244
Fat: 8 g
Protein: 16 g

Sodium: 229 mg
Fiber: 3 g
Carbohydrates: 28 g
Sugar: 23 g

PINEAPPLE TVP BAKED BEANS

Add a splash of the tropics to the sweet and tangy flavor of traditional baked beans. The TVP adds protein to keep you fuller longer, and the pineapple enhances the sweetness of the barbecue sauce without being overpowering.

SERVES 4

2 (15-ounce) cans black beans, partially drained

1 medium yellow onion, peeled and diced

2/3 cup barbecue sauce

2 tablespoons yellow mustard

2 tablespoons light brown sugar

1 cup TVP

1 cup hot water

1 (8-ounce) can diced pineapple, drained

1/4 teaspoon salt

1/2 teaspoon ground black pepper

1. In a large saucepan over low heat, bring beans, onion, barbecue sauce, mustard, and brown sugar to a simmer (liquid should be moving, but no bubbles should be forming). Cover and cook for 10 minutes.

2. Mix TVP with hot water and let sit for 7 minutes to rehydrate. Drain well.

3. Add TVP, pineapple, salt, and pepper to bean mixture, and simmer for another 12 minutes. Then, thanks to the TVP, you'll be saying TTYL to hunger!

Per Serving:
Calories: 481
Fat: 2 g
Protein: 31 g

Sodium: 701 mg
Fiber: 23 g
Carbohydrates: 87 g
Sugar: 31 g

CHAPTER 7

CLASSIC MAIN DISHES: VEGAN TWISTS ON FAMILIAR FAVORITES

BECAUSE EATING VEGAN DOESN'T MEAN GIVING UP THAT COMFORT FOOD

BEER-BATTERED
TOFU FILLET

Who needs eggs when beer is sticky enough to hold any batter? No one, that's who.

SERVES 8

2 teaspoons garlic powder

2 teaspoons onion powder

2 teaspoons paprika

1 teaspoon salt

1/2 teaspoon ground black pepper

3 (1-pound) blocks extra-firm tofu, chopped chunky

1 (12-ounce) bottle vegan beer

1 1/2 cups whole-wheat flour

1/4 cup canola oil

1. In a small bowl, mix garlic powder, onion powder, paprika, salt, and pepper. Lightly pat pieces of tofu in mixture, making sure it sticks.

2. Pour beer into a large bowl and add flour. Stir well. Dip tofu into beer batter.

3. In a medium skillet, heat oil for 30 seconds over medium heat, then sauté tofu for about 3 minutes until crispy and crunchy on all sides.

Per Serving:
Calories: 217
Fat: 11 g
Protein: 9 g

Sodium: 296 mg
Fiber: 4 g
Carbohydrates: 20 g
Sugar: 0 g

TOFU "FISH" STICKS

The seaweed in this recipe lends a fishlike taste for all you seafarers out there. Please, do have a whale of a time with this recipe—it's fabulous!

SERVES 3

½ cup white whole-wheat flour

½ cup unsweetened soy milk

2 tablespoons lemon juice

2 tablespoons dulse seaweed flakes

1 tablespoon Old Bay Seasoning

1 teaspoon onion powder

1½ cups finely ground bread crumbs

1 (1-pound) block extra-firm tofu, well pressed and sliced into ½"-thick strips

1. Preheat oven to 350°F.
2. Set up three small bowls. Place flour in one. Add milk and lemon juice to the second. In the third, mix together seaweed flakes, Old Bay Seasoning, onion powder, and bread crumbs.
3. Coat each tofu strip with flour, dip into milk mixture, then dip into bread crumb mixture.
4. Place strips on a baking sheet lightly greased with vegan margarine, and bake for 20 minutes, turning over once halfway through cooking. Serve with ketchup!

Per Serving:
Calories: 381
Fat: 11 g
Protein: 23 g

Sodium: 434 mg
Fiber: 5 g
Carbohydrates: 43 g
Sugar: 5 g

TOFU BBQ SAUCE "STEAKS"

Tofu "steaks" are perfect for a mock roast beef sandwich. Perhaps you are just in the mood to eat some meat. Urges happen. So go ahead: you could fool anyone with flavor like this!

SERVES 4

¼ cup barbecue sauce

¼ cup water

2 teaspoons balsamic vinegar

2 tablespoons soy sauce

2 tablespoons hot sauce

2 teaspoons granulated sugar

½ medium yellow onion, peeled and chopped

2 tablespoons olive oil

2 (1-pound) blocks extra-firm tofu, pressed and sliced into ½"-thick strips

1. Whisk together barbecue sauce, water, vinegar, soy sauce, hot sauce, and sugar in a small bowl. Set aside.

2. In a large saucepan over medium-high heat, sauté onion in oil for 3 minutes. Add tofu. Fry until tofu is golden, about 2 minutes on each side.

3. Lower the heat to medium, and add sauce mixture. Coat tofu and stir for about 6 minutes until sauce thickens. Eat up!

Per Serving:
Calories: 223
Fat: 13 g
Protein: 13 g

Sodium: 728 mg
Fiber: 2 g
Carbohydrates: 14 g
Sugar: 9 g

BASIC HOMEMADE SEITAN

Homemade seitan is less expensive than store-bought. It takes a while to cook, but it's a good option if you're interested in creating your own from scratch and saving it for later use. After all, homemade is always better than store-bought.

SERVES 8

1 cup vital wheat gluten

1 teaspoon onion powder

1 teaspoon garlic powder

6¾ cups strong vegetable broth, divided

2 tablespoons soy sauce

1. In a medium bowl, mix together wheat gluten, onion powder, and garlic powder. In a different small bowl, mix ¾ cup broth and soy sauce.
2. Slowly add broth mixture to wheat gluten mixture, kneading with your hands until wheat gluten forms a ball of dough.
3. Continue kneading dough until the texture is universally smooth. Allow to sit for a few minutes, then knead again for 3 minutes.
4. Divide dough into 4½"-thick pieces.
5. In a large stockpot over medium heat, bring 6 cups broth to a simmer (liquid should be moving, but no bubbles should be forming). Add dough pieces and continue to simmer for 1 hour on low heat.
6. Drain broth and save seitan for later in the refrigerator, or add to your favorite seitan dish. Seitan can be stored in the refrigerator for up to 1 week and in the freezer for up to 1 month.

Per Serving:
Calories: 62
Fat: 0 g
Protein: 12 g

Sodium: 317 mg
Fiber: 0 g
Carbohydrates: 3 g
Sugar: 0 g

BRAISED TOFU AND VEGGIE CACCIATORE

Delicious over pasta or rice. Brown rice would be a perfect complement along with a nice glass (or two...or three...) of red wine.

SERVES 4

½ medium yellow onion, peeled and chopped

½ cup sliced white mushrooms

1 medium carrot, peeled and chopped

3 cloves garlic, peeled and minced

2 (1-pound) blocks extra-firm tofu, chopped into cubes

2 tablespoons olive oil

½ cup white cooking wine

3 large tomatoes, diced

1 (6-ounce) can tomato paste

1 bay leaf

½ teaspoon salt

1 teaspoon dried parsley leaves

1 teaspoon dried oregano leaves

1 teaspoon dried basil leaves

1. In a large saucepan over medium-high heat, sauté onion, mushrooms, carrot, garlic, and tofu in oil for 5 minutes.

2. Reduce heat to medium-low, and add wine, tomatoes, tomato paste, bay leaf, salt, and remaining spices. Stir up well. It'll smell heavenly.

3. Cover the pan and let simmer for 20 minutes. Stir every once in a while, and don't forget to take out the bay leaf before eating.

Per Serving:
Calories: 380
Fat: 19 g
Protein: 27 g

Sodium: 845 mg
Fiber: 7 g
Carbohydrates: 23 g
Sugar: 11 g

SOUTHERN-FRIED SEITAN

Veganism can be healthy. But it can also be decadent. Deep-fried seitan is as good as any chicken-fried steak.

SERVES 4

2 tablespoons soy sauce

1/4 cup unsweetened soy milk

2 tablespoons yellow mustard

2/3 cup white whole-wheat flour

1/4 cup nutritional yeast

1 tablespoon baking powder

1 teaspoon garlic powder

1 teaspoon onion powder

1/2 teaspoon paprika

1/2 teaspoon salt

1/2 teaspoon ground black pepper

1 (16-ounce) package seitan

1/4 cup canola oil

1. In a small bowl, mix soy sauce, milk, and mustard.
2. In another small bowl, mix remaining ingredients except seitan and oil. Coat seitan pieces first in milk mixture, then in flour mixture.
3. In a medium saucepan over medium heat, heat oil for 30 seconds. Fry seitan until golden brown, about 4 minutes total. Drain on paper towels before serving.

Per Serving:
Calories: 255
Fat: 7 g
Protein: 25 g

Sodium: 1,288 mg
Fiber: 4 g
Carbohydrates: 26 g
Sugar: 2 g

HOMEMADE BAKED BBQ SEITAN

In this recipe you bake, rather than boil, the homemade seitan. This version is warm right out of the oven. It yields a "lunch meat"–style seitan that can be sliced and put into sandwiches!

SERVES 8

1 (12-ounce) block silken tofu

²/₃ cup water

¹/₃ cup olive oil

¹/₃ cup barbecue sauce

2 teaspoons hot sauce

1 teaspoon onion powder

1 teaspoon garlic powder

1 teaspoon seasoning salt

¹/₄ cup vital wheat gluten

1. Preheat oven to 350°F.
2. Purée tofu, water, and oil for 1 minute in a food processor. Add barbecue sauce, hot sauce, onion powder, garlic powder, and seasoning salt to mixture.
3. Place mixture in a large bowl. Add vital wheat gluten, then form a dough by kneading with your hands. Knead until dough is universally smooth. Let sit for 3 minutes, then knead again for 2 minutes.
4. Press dough into a 9" × 5" loaf pan greased with vegan margarine. Bake for 40 minutes. Cut and serve.

Per Serving:
Calories: 139
Fat: 10 g
Protein: 5 g

Sodium: 233 mg
Fiber: 0 g
Carbohydrates: 7 g
Sugar: 4 g

"CHICKENY" SEITAN

If you add in vegan chicken bouillon cubes, seitan will take on a chicken-like flavor. It's perfect for when you're craving a meal of chicken but are still in the mood to stick to your vegan guns.

SERVES 8

1 cup vital wheat gluten

1 tablespoon nutritional yeast

1/2 teaspoon dried sage

1/2 teaspoon dried thyme leaves

1/2 teaspoon garlic powder

1/2 teaspoon onion powder

6³/₄ cups vegetable broth, divided

1. Mix wheat gluten, nutritional yeast, sage, thyme, garlic powder, and onion powder in a medium bowl.

2. Add ³/₄ cup broth to mixture, and combine with your hands. Knead mixture into a smooth dough. Let sit for 3 minutes, then knead again for 2 minutes. Divide dough into 4¹/₂"-thick pieces.

3. In a large stockpot over low heat, heat remaining broth about 10 minutes. Add dough pieces and simmer 1 hour. Use this seitan in Not-Chicken Soup (see recipe in Chapter 5) or on top of a salad.

Per Serving:
Calories: 60
Fat: 0 g
Protein: 12 g

Sodium: 67 mg
Fiber: 0 g
Carbohydrates: 3 g
Sugar: 0 g

SUPER-MEATY TVP MEATLOAF

TVP stands for "textured vegetable protein," or soy protein "meat"—slightly unappealing, but this recipe does meatloaf justice. Plus, it's low in fat! This delicious recipe will yet again surprise your tongue with the tasty flexibility of veganism.

SERVES 6

2 cups TVP

1³/₄ cups hot vegetable broth

1 medium yellow onion, peeled and chopped

1 tablespoon canola oil

¹/₄ cup ketchup

¹/₂ cup plus 3 tablespoons barbecue sauce, divided

1 cup vital wheat gluten

1 cup bread crumbs

1 teaspoon dried parsley leaves

¹/₂ teaspoon dried sage

¹/₂ teaspoon salt

¹/₄ teaspoon ground black pepper

1. In a medium bowl, combine TVP with hot broth to rehydrate. Let sit for 7 minutes. Squeeze out excess moisture.
2. In a small saucepan over medium heat, sauté onion in oil for about 4 minutes until translucent.
3. Preheat oven to 400°F.
4. In a large bowl, mix TVP, sautéed onion, ketchup, and ¹/₂ cup barbecue sauce. Add vital wheat gluten, bread crumbs, and spices.
5. Press mixture into a 9" × 5" loaf pan greased with vegan margarine, and pour remaining 3 tablespoons barbecue sauce over top. Cook for 45 minutes. Allow to cool for 10 minutes before attempting to cut.

Per Serving:
Calories: 348
Fat: 4 g
Protein: 34 g

Sodium: 949 mg
Fiber: 7 g
Carbohydrates: 43 g
Sugar: 19 g

TVP "SLOPPY JOES"

Kids love these sloppy joes. And they have no idea that their yummy sandwiches are full of vegany goodness. Serve on bulky whole-wheat rolls with Baked Zucchini Fries (see recipe in Chapter 3)!

SERVES 8

1¾ cups TVP

1 cup hot water

1 medium yellow onion, peeled and chopped

1 medium green bell pepper, seeded and diced

2 tablespoons olive oil

1 (16-ounce) can tomato sauce

¼ cup barbecue sauce

2 tablespoons chili powder

1 tablespoon mustard powder

1 tablespoon soy sauce

2 tablespoons molasses

2 tablespoons apple cider vinegar

1 teaspoon hot sauce

1 teaspoon garlic powder

½ teaspoon salt

1. In a medium bowl, mix TVP with hot water. Let sit for 7 minutes, then drain.
2. In a large stockpot over medium-high heat, sauté onion and bell pepper in oil for 3 minutes.
3. Reduce heat to medium-low, and add TVP and all remaining ingredients. Cover and let simmer for 15 minutes. Check back occasionally to stir.

Per Serving:
Calories: 166
Fat: 4 g
Protein: 12 g

Sodium: 694 mg
Fiber: 6 g
Carbohydrates: 20 g
Sugar: 13 g

SEITAN BARBECUE "MEAT"

Have the winter blues and wish you were lazily hanging out on your porch in July? Sadly you can't change the weather, but you can always change up some flavors to pretend you're living in a summertime wonderland. A little delusion never hurt anybody...

SERVES 6

1 (1-pound) package seitan, sliced into thin strips

1 large yellow onion, peeled and chopped

3 cloves garlic, peeled and minced

2 tablespoons olive oil

1 cup barbecue sauce

2 tablespoons water

6 sourdough bread rolls, toasted

1 medium head lettuce, shredded

1 medium tomato, sliced

6 tablespoons Vegan Mayonnaise (see recipe in Chapter 4)

1. In a medium saucepan over medium-low heat, heat seitan, onion, and garlic in oil. Stir continuously for about 4 minutes.
2. Reduce heat to medium-low, and add in barbecue sauce and water. Let simmer and stir frequently for 10 minutes.
3. Fill each roll with equal parts barbecue seitan, lettuce, tomato, and Vegan Mayonnaise!

Per Serving:
Calories: 422
Fat: 10 g
Protein: 21 g

Sodium: 1,053 mg
Fiber: 4 g
Carbohydrates: 63 g
Sugar: 21 g

TVP-STUFFED PEPPERS

There is nothing like warm peppers piping with protein and goodness. They make a colorful and clever presentation for a hearty meal. Your friends won't miss the meat!

SERVES 6

3/4 cup TVP

3/4 cup hot vegetable broth

1 medium yellow onion, peeled and chopped

2 ribs celery, diced

2/3 cup chopped white mushrooms

2 tablespoons olive oil

1 1/2 cups cooked brown rice

1 teaspoon chopped fresh Italian flat-leaf parsley

1/2 teaspoon dried oregano leaves

1/2 teaspoon salt

2 cups marinara sauce, divided

6 medium red bell peppers, sliced in half lengthwise and seeded

1. Preheat oven to 325°F.
2. Combine TVP and hot broth in a small bowl to rehydrate. Let sit for 7 minutes, then drain.
3. In a large saucepan over medium heat, cook onion, celery, and mushrooms for 5 minutes in oil until mushrooms are browned. Reduce heat to medium-low, and add rehydrated TVP, rice, parsley, oregano, salt, and 1 1/2 cups marinara sauce. Mix well.
4. Stuff mixture into bell peppers, and set in an ungreased 9" × 13" casserole dish. Cover with remaining 1/2 cup marinara sauce and cook for 30 minutes.

Per Serving:
Calories: 236
Fat: 7 g
Protein: 10 g

Sodium: 680 mg
Fiber: 7 g
Carbohydrates: 33 g
Sugar: 12 g

TEMPEH DILL "CHICKEN" SALAD

What would a backyard barbecue be without chicken salad? Let's not find out.

SERVES 6

2 (8-ounce) packages tempeh, diced small

1 cup water

6 tablespoons Vegan Mayonnaise (see recipe in Chapter 4)

2 tablespoons lemon juice

½ teaspoon garlic powder

1 teaspoon Dijon mustard

2 tablespoons sweet pickle relish

½ cup frozen green peas, thawed

2 ribs celery, diced small

1 tablespoon chopped fresh dill

1. In a medium saucepan over medium-low heat, combine tempeh and water, and let simmer for 10 minutes. Drain.
2. Whisk together Vegan Mayonnaise, lemon juice, garlic powder, mustard, and relish in a medium bowl.
3. In a large bowl, mix drained tempeh, Vegan Mayonnaise mixture, peas, celery, and dill. Toss.
4. Chill covered for 1 hour, and serve!

Per Serving:
Calories: 194
Fat: 11 g
Protein: 17 g

Sodium: 128 mg
Fiber: 1 g
Carbohydrates: 11 g
Sugar: 3 g

TVP, MUSHROOM, AND WHITE WINE STROGANOFF

A stroganoff is a creamy and rich Russian dish typically served over potatoes, pasta, or rice. Serve yours however you like—just don't forget the vodka cocktails!

SERVES 4

¾ cup TVP

¾ cup hot vegetable broth

1 medium yellow onion, peeled and diced

1½ cups sliced white mushrooms

2 tablespoons vegan margarine

½ cup white wine

½ teaspoon dried sage

½ teaspoon chopped fresh Italian flat-leaf parsley

½ teaspoon garlic powder

1 tablespoon white whole-wheat flour

2 cups unsweetened soy milk

½ cup nondairy sour cream

2 tablespoons Dijon mustard

⅛ teaspoon salt

⅛ teaspoon ground black pepper

1. In a small bowl, mix TVP and hot broth to rehydrate. Let sit for about 7 minutes. Drain.
2. In a large skillet over medium heat, cook onion and mushrooms in margarine for about 2 minutes. Add wine, sage, parsley, and garlic powder. Simmer for 4 minutes over medium-low heat.
3. Add in flour and stir continuously so sauce thickens. Slowly add in milk, whisking to combine.
4. Add sour cream and mustard. Stir until well combined. Mix in TVP. Season with salt and pepper, and serve.

Per Serving:
Calories: 295
Fat: 13 g
Protein: 15 g

Sodium: 624 mg
Fiber: 5 g
Carbohydrates: 22 g
Sugar: 9 g

SPAGHETTI SQUASH DINNER

Veggie pasta is a delicious staple. Using a food processor, you can grate carrots or zucchini into pasta-like shapes, plummeting your caloric intake while still enjoying your favorite macaroni dishes. In this case spaghetti squash, when cooked, scrapes out into the shape of noodles all by itself!

SERVES 2

1 medium spaghetti squash, halved and seeded

2 tablespoons olive oil

⅛ teaspoon salt

⅛ teaspoon ground black pepper

⅛ teaspoon garlic powder

¼ cup balsamic vinegar

¼ cup red wine

1 medium yellow tomato, diced

½ cup marinara sauce

2 tablespoons nutritional yeast

1. Preheat oven to 400°F.
2. Brush inside of squash with oil, and season with salt, pepper, and garlic powder. Place facedown on an ungreased baking sheet. Cook for 45 minutes.
3. In a small bowl, combine vinegar and wine. Add tomato and marinara sauce and let marinate while squash cooks.
4. Remove squash from oven. Let cool for 10 minutes. With a fork, scrape out the insides of squash. Divide into 2 bowls.
5. Pour sauce mixture over "spaghetti," and sprinkle with nutritional yeast.

Per Serving:
Calories: 440
Fat: 17 g
Protein: 9 g

Sodium: 591 mg
Fiber: 14 g
Carbohydrates: 65 g
Sugar: 29 g

SO INCREDIBLY EASY BLACK BEAN BURGERS

Simple burgers that don't fall apart. Go along with the summer feel and serve these burgers with lemonade and an easy vegan potato salad.

YIELDS 6 PATTIES

- 1 (15-ounce) can black beans, drained
- 3 tablespoons dried minced onions
- 1 teaspoon salt
- 1½ teaspoons garlic powder
- 2 teaspoons chopped fresh Italian flat-leaf parsley
- 1 teaspoon chili powder
- ⅔ cup white whole-wheat flour
- ¼ cup canola oil

1. Process black beans in a food processor until partially blended.
2. Transfer beans to a medium bowl. Add in onions and all spices. Mash up with a fork to combine.
3. Add flour in slowly, continuing to mash with a fork. Form into patties.
4. In a medium skillet over medium heat, add oil and heat for 30 seconds. Add black bean patties and cook for 3 minutes on each side. You don't want them soft on the inside, so make certain to cook them for the full 6 minutes.

Per Serving: 1 patty
Calories: 156
Fat: 6 g
Protein: 6 g

Sodium: 519 mg
Fiber: 6 g
Carbohydrates: 21 g
Sugar: 1 g

NO SHEPHERD, NO SHEEP PIE

There is absolutely nothing more comforting on this earth than a nice, hot, steaming slice of shepherd's pie—until now. This secretly vegan version will warm your guests to their toes and heat hearts for lively discussions around the table.

SERVES 6

1½ cups TVP

1½ cups hot vegetable broth

½ medium yellow onion, peeled and chopped

2 cloves garlic, peeled and minced

1 large carrot, peeled and sliced thin

2 tablespoons olive oil

¾ cup sliced white mushrooms

½ cup frozen green peas, thawed

½ cup vegetable broth, room temperature

½ cup plus 3 tablespoons unsweetened soy milk, divided

1 tablespoon white whole-wheat flour

5 medium red potatoes, peeled and cooked

2 tablespoons vegan margarine

¼ teaspoon dried rosemary leaves

½ teaspoon dried sage

½ teaspoon salt

¼ teaspoon ground black pepper

1. Preheat oven to 350°F.
2. In a medium bowl, mix TVP with hot broth, and let sit for 7 minutes. Drain.
3. In a medium skillet over medium-high heat, sauté onion, garlic, and carrot in oil for 5 minutes. Add mushrooms, peas, ½ cup broth at room temperature, and ½ cup milk. Add flour and let sauce thicken up. Move mixture into a greased 9" × 13" casserole dish.
4. In a large bowl, mash potatoes, margarine, and remaining 3 tablespoons milk with rosemary, sage, salt, and pepper. Spread over vegetables in dish.
5. Bake for 35 minutes. Enjoy, mate!

Per Serving:
Calories: 198
Fat: 9 g
Protein: 14 g

Sodium: 486 mg
Fiber: 5 g
Carbohydrates: 15 g
Sugar: 6 g

SPICY SOUTHERN JAMBALAYA

Pack away the rest for leftovers. Making a big rice dish and then eating it throughout the week saves time and hassle. Plus, this dish will jump-start your taste buds every time.

SERVES 6

2 tablespoons olive oil

1 medium yellow bell pepper, seeded and chopped

1 medium yellow onion, peeled and chopped

1 (14-ounce) can diced tomatoes, undrained

3 cups vegetable broth

2 cups brown rice

1 bay leaf

1 teaspoon paprika

1/2 teaspoon dried thyme leaves

1/2 teaspoon dried oregano leaves

1/2 teaspoon garlic powder

1 cup frozen corn, thawed

1/2 teaspoon cayenne pepper

1/2 teaspoon hot sauce

1. In a large stockpot over medium heat, heat oil for 30 seconds. Add bell pepper and cook for 1 minute. Add onion and cook for another 3 minutes until soft.

2. Reduce heat from medium to low, and add remaining ingredients except cayenne pepper and hot sauce. Simmer, covered, for 20 minutes.

3. Add cayenne pepper and hot sauce to the pot. Mix through. Let spice settle for about 3 minutes, then remove from heat. Remove bay leaf and admire your work.

PART-TIME TIP

Brown rice has more fiber than white rice because the bran of the grain remains. If you want a more filling dish, try adding some kidney beans. You can even add pieces of a whole-grain baguette as makeshift croutons! Just be sure to add it right after taking the jambalaya off the stove, and serve immediately.

Per Serving:
Calories: 357
Fat: 7 g
Protein: 8 g

Sodium: 464 mg
Fiber: 6 g
Carbohydrates: 37 g
Sugar: 6 g

HAWAIIAN PINEAPPLE AND MINT RICE

Have a little cabin fever? Try a little island fever. This rice dish is refreshing and sweet—something that will cool you off on a hot day. So close your eyes, take a bite, and imagine you're on an island holiday, surrounded by the lapping waves of the Pacific.

SERVES 6

4 cups cooked white rice

$\frac{1}{2}$ cup chopped macadamia nuts

1 cup diced fresh pineapple

$\frac{1}{2}$ cup raisins

$\frac{1}{4}$ cup dried papaya

$\frac{1}{3}$ cup pineapple juice

2 tablespoons olive oil

2 tablespoons red wine vinegar

$\frac{1}{4}$ cup toasted coconut flakes

2 tablespoons chopped fresh mint

1. Mix rice, nuts, pineapple, raisins, and papaya in a large bowl. Set aside.
2. In a small bowl, whisk together pineapple juice, oil, and vinegar. Add to rice mixture. Chill covered for $1\frac{1}{2}$ hours.
3. Only add coconut and mint right before serving so they don't get soggy!

Per Serving:
Calories: 349
Fat: 15 g
Protein: 5 g

Sodium: 407 mg
Fiber: 3 g
Carbohydrates: 52 g
Sugar: 16 g

CRANBERRY APPLE WILD RICE

A delicious mix of sweet and salty, this recipe can be reworked as a great breakfast dish. Just replace the vegetable broth with almond or soy milk; the salt and pepper with brown sugar and cinnamon; the olive oil with honey; and the scallions, onions, and celery with raisins.

SERVES 4

1 medium red onion, peeled and diced

2 tablespoons olive oil

1 cup wild rice

3 cups vegetable broth

1/3 cup no-pulp orange juice

1/2 cup dried cranberries

1/2 cup raw almonds

2 scallions, chopped

1 large red apple, peeled and diced

1/8 teaspoon salt

1/8 teaspoon ground black pepper

1. In a large saucepan over medium-high heat, sauté onion in oil for about 3 minutes.
2. Reduce heat to low. Add rice and broth. Simmer, covered, for 30 minutes. Add orange juice and simmer, covered, for another 15 minutes.
3. Remove from heat, add cranberries, and let sit for 5 minutes. Toss in remaining ingredients and serve.

Per Serving:
Calories: 447
Fat: 17 g
Protein: 11 g

Sodium: 573 mg
Fiber: 8 g
Carbohydrates: 69g
Sugar: 26 g

YOU BETTER BELIEVE IT: BAKED MAC 'N' CHEESE

Dairy-free mac 'n' cheese for all the vegan doubters out there. Add peas, broccoli florets, or spinach and diced tomatoes for even more flavor.

SERVES 6

1 (12-ounce) package whole-wheat macaroni

1 (1-pound) block silken tofu

1 cup plain unsweetened almond milk

1 teaspoon Homemade Tahini (see recipe in Chapter 3)

1 tablespoon lemon juice

1/2 teaspoon apple cider vinegar

1 tablespoon miso

1/4 cup nutritional yeast

1 teaspoon garlic powder

1 teaspoon onion powder

1 teaspoon ground white pepper

2 tablespoons vegan margarine

1 cup whole-wheat bread crumbs

1/2 teaspoon salt

1/2 teaspoon paprika

1/2 teaspoon ground nutmeg

1. Preheat oven to 350°F.
2. Prepare macaroni according to package directions, drain, and place into an ungreased 9" × 13" casserole dish.
3. Purée tofu, milk, tahini, lemon juice, vinegar, miso, nutritional yeast, garlic powder, onion powder, and white pepper in a food processor. Make certain to blend well.
4. Pour "cheese" sauce over macaroni in the casserole dish.
5. In a small saucepan over medium-high heat, melt margarine for 30 seconds and mix in bread crumbs, stirring so nothing burns. Spread bread crumbs over macaroni.
6. Top macaroni with salt, paprika, and nutmeg. Bake for 25 minutes, and dig in!

Per Serving:
Calories: 371
Fat: 9 g
Protein: 16 g

Sodium: 518 mg
Fiber: 6 g
Carbohydrates: 60 g
Sugar: 4 g

PUMPKIN CREAM PASTA

This sauce, which tastes so richly of autumn, also makes a great dipping sauce for hot garlic breadsticks. You'll be smiling like a jack-o'-lantern by the time you're through.

SERVES 4

- 2 tablespoons vegan margarine
- 1 medium yellow onion, peeled and chopped
- 2 cloves garlic, peeled and minced
- 1½ cups soy cream
- 1 (15-ounce) can puréed pumpkin
- ½ cup nutritional yeast
- ½ teaspoon chopped fresh Italian flat-leaf parsley
- ⅛ teaspoon salt
- ⅛ teaspoon ground black pepper
- 2 cups cooked whole-wheat pasta

1. In a large saucepan over medium-high heat, melt margarine for 30 seconds. Add onion and garlic, and cook for about 4 minutes.

2. Lower heat to medium. Add cream and pumpkin, and stir. Cook for 10 minutes, stirring frequently to ensure that ingredients blend smoothly.

3. Add remaining ingredients except pasta, letting cook for another 2 minutes. Pour over pasta and serve.

Per Serving:
Calories: 367
Fat: 22 g
Protein: 11 g

Sodium: 204 mg
Fiber: 7 g
Carbohydrates: 34 g
Sugar: 6 g

BAKED MILLET PATTIES

Nutty and delicious, wholesome and nutritious. Eat this dish topped with a whole-grain bun and a slice of vegan cheese. Add some grilled red onions, a little honey mustard, and hummus, and there you go!

YIELDS 8 PATTIES

1½ cups cooked millet

½ cup Homemade Tahini (see recipe in Chapter 3)

1 teaspoon chopped fresh Italian flat-leaf parsley

¾ teaspoon garlic powder

½ teaspoon onion powder

½ teaspoon salt

1. Preheat oven to 350°F.
2. Mix all ingredients in a medium bowl, mashing up well. Form into 8 patties, and place on an ungreased baking sheet.
3. Cook for 10 minutes on each side.

THE SKINNY ON...VEGAN CHEESE

There are several kinds of vegan cheese slices available, usually made from ingredients like rice, soy, almond, or vegetables. Most of these options are extremely low in fat as well! They're perfect for grilled cheese or burgers like these. There are so many flavors available—mozzarella, Cheddar, American, pepper jack—that you're certain to find a favorite.

Per Serving: 1 patty
Calories: 138
Fat: 10 g
Protein: 3 g

Sodium: 169 mg
Fiber: 2 g
Carbohydrates: 11 g
Sugar: 0 g

BARLEY AND MUSHROOM PILAF

Hello, pilaf! It's a dish cooked in a rich broth and aromatic seasonings. Make certain to buy pearl barley: it cooks in just 20 minutes.

SERVES 4

3 tablespoons vegan margarine, divided

1 cup sliced porcini mushrooms

1 cup sliced shiitake mushrooms

2 ribs celery, diced

1/2 medium yellow onion, peeled and chopped

1 1/4 cups barley

3 3/4 cups vegetable broth

1 bay leaf

1/4 teaspoon dried sage

1/2 teaspoon chopped fresh Italian flat-leaf parsley

1/2 teaspoon dried thyme leaves

1. In a large stockpot over medium-high heat, melt 2 tablespoons margarine for 30 seconds. Sauté both kinds of mushrooms, celery, and onion for 3 minutes. Add barley and remaining 1 tablespoon of margarine. Stir frequently and cook for about 3 more minutes.

2. When barley is toasted and has a brownish tint, add broth and remaining spices. Cover and cook for 25 minutes. Stir every now and then, and remember to take out the bay leaf before eating.

Per Serving:
Calories: 323
Fat: 9 g
Protein: 8 g

Sodium: 728 mg
Fiber: 11 g
Carbohydrates: 54 g
Sugar: 3 g

SUMMER SQUASH AND BARLEY RISOTTO

When summer is curving into autumn, use the last of the bright summer squash while you still can. Ideal for stir-fries and an excellent and colorful mix-in for any grain dish, it adds a fresh, crisp flavor. Add some porcini mushrooms and asparagus for more variety!

SERVES 4

- 2 cloves garlic, peeled and minced
- ½ medium yellow onion, peeled and diced
- 1 medium zucchini, chopped
- 1 medium yellow squash, chopped
- 2 tablespoons olive oil
- 1 cup barley
- 3 cups vegetable broth, divided
- 2 tablespoons chopped fresh basil
- 2 tablespoons vegan margarine
- 2 tablespoons nutritional yeast
- ⅛ teaspoon salt
- ⅛ teaspoon ground black pepper

1. In a large saucepan over medium-high heat, sauté garlic, onion, zucchini, and squash in oil for 4 minutes. Add barley, stirring frequently, and cook for 1 minute until browned and toasted.

2. Add in 1 cup broth. Bring to a simmer (liquid should be moving, but no bubbles should be forming), then cover for about 4 minutes until all liquid is absorbed. Add in 1 more cup broth, cover, and cook for 25 minutes.

3. When barley is all cooked through, add remaining broth and basil, stirring until heated.

4. Remove from heat and mix in margarine, nutritional yeast, salt, and pepper. Serve warm.

THE SKINNY ON...RISOTTO

Risotto is a dish cooked with a grain (usually rice) and simmered until very rich and creamy. Try using all different types of grains—it's time to experiment! There's bulgur wheat, millet, barley, quinoa, and so many kinds of rice you probably haven't even heard of.

Per Serving:
Calories: 326
Fat: 13 g
Protein: 8 g

Sodium: 640 mg
Fiber: 9 g
Carbohydrates: 46 g
Sugar: 4 g

MILLET AND BUTTERNUT SQUASH CASSEROLE

This is a great autumn dish after all the summer squashes have waved goodbye for the duration of the cold months.

SERVES 4

1 cup millet

2 cups vegetable broth

1 small butternut squash, peeled, seeded, and chopped

½ cup water

1 teaspoon curry powder

½ cup no-pulp orange juice

½ teaspoon salt

2 tablespoons nutritional yeast

¼ cup chopped raw almonds

1. In a large saucepan over medium heat, cook millet in broth for 20 minutes.
2. In another large pan, place squash in water, covering and cooking for 20 minutes over medium heat. You want squash to be soft. Drain.
3. Turn heat to low and mix in millet. Add curry powder and orange juice, stirring to combine. Cook for another 4 minutes.
4. Remove from heat, and mix in salt and nutritional yeast. Top with almonds.

Per Serving:
Calories: 345
Fat: 5 g
Protein: 10 g

Sodium: 634 mg
Fiber: 8 g
Carbohydrates: 69 g
Sugar: 9 g

QUINOA MAC 'N' "CHEESE"

Delicious, full of protein, mixed with veggies, and not a heavy cheese or milk ingredient in sight! You might just ask yourself why you've never done this before. Try this dish on your non-vegan friends and dare them to tell you they don't like it. This one is a winner.

SERVES 4

3 cups vegetable broth

1½ cups quinoa

1 medium yellow onion, peeled and chopped

3 cloves garlic, peeled and minced

2 tablespoons olive oil

1 bunch fresh broccoli, diced

1 large tomato, diced

1 tablespoon whole-wheat flour

¾ cup unsweetened soy milk

½ teaspoon salt

1 cup shredded vegan cheese

1 cup seasoned bread crumbs

½ teaspoon dried parsley leaves

½ teaspoon ground nutmeg

1. Preheat oven to 350°F.
2. In a large stockpot over high heat, bring broth to a boil, and then turn heat down to simmer on low. Add quinoa. Cover and let cook for 20 minutes.
3. In a large saucepan over medium heat, sauté onion and garlic in oil for about 4 minutes. Add broccoli and tomato, and cook for an additional 4 minutes.
4. Add flour to onion mixture, and then add milk and salt. Continue mixing until sauce is thickened, about 3 minutes.
5. In an ungreased 9" × 13" casserole dish, mix quinoa and onion mixture together. Add cheese and mix thoroughly. Sprinkle bread crumbs, parsley, and nutmeg over top. Bake 12 minutes.

Per Serving:	
Calories: 582	Sodium: 1,247 mg
Fat: 21 g	Fiber: 12 g
Protein: 21 g	Carbohydrates: 83 g
	Sugar: 11 g

CARAMELIZED ONION AND BARBECUE SAUCE PIZZA

Sweet, tangy, and packed with protein thanks to the tofu. Try making this dish with whole-grain pizza dough for an even more filling meal. This recipe will prove that you don't need cheese to make a great pizza!

SERVES 4

- $2/3$ cup barbecue sauce
- 1 (9") vegan pizza crust or pizza dough
- 2 medium red onions, peeled and chopped
- 3 tablespoons olive oil
- 1 (1-pound) block firm tofu, diced
- $1/2$ cup diced canned pineapple, drained
- $1/3$ teaspoon garlic powder
- $1/8$ teaspoon salt
- $1/8$ teaspoon ground black pepper

1. Preheat oven to 450°F.
2. Spread barbecue sauce over pizza crust. If you bought a premade crust, simply put it onto the oven rack as is. If you purchased dough, lightly grease a 9" × 13" pan with vegan margarine, and smooth dough in the pan before adding barbecue sauce.
3. In a medium skillet over medium heat, sauté onions in oil for 4 minutes. Add tofu, and continue cooking until tofu is crisped and onions are translucent.
4. Top pizza with tofu, onions, and pineapple. Sprinkle with garlic powder, salt, and pepper.
5. Bake for approximately 14 minutes. Pizza is done when bottom of crust is lightly browned.

Per Serving:
Calories: 448
Fat: 18 g
Protein: 16 g

Sodium: 984 mg
Fiber: 4 g
Carbohydrates: 55 g
Sugar: 21 g

CAJUN-SPICED CORNMEAL-BREADED TOFU

A recipe that brings to mind breaded catfish. There is not a way in the world you'll be able to say no to this spicy Cajun recipe. In fact, "spicy" and "Cajun" should be synonymous with "delicious." Serve with hot sauce or barbecue sauce.

SERVES 3

²/₃ cup unsweetened soy milk

2 tablespoons lime juice

¹/₄ cup white whole-wheat flour

¹/₃ cup cornmeal

1 tablespoon Cajun seasoning

1 teaspoon onion powder

¹/₂ teaspoon salt

¹/₂ teaspoon ground black pepper

¹/₂ teaspoon cayenne pepper

1 (1-pound) block firm tofu, well pressed and cut into strips

¹/₄ cup canola oil

1. Preheat oven to 350°F. Grease a 9" × 13" baking dish with vegan margarine. (Or you will be very sad come eatin' time.)
2. In a large, shallow bowl, combine milk and lime juice. Whisk well.
3. In another large bowl, mix flour, cornmeal, Cajun seasoning, onion powder, salt, black pepper, and cayenne pepper.
4. Dip tofu strips one at a time in milk mixture and then coat with flour mixture.
5. Add strips to the baking dish, and cook for 10 minutes.

Per Serving:
Calories: 362
Fat: 24 g
Protein: 17 g

Sodium: 419 mg
Fiber: 4 g
Carbohydrates: 21 g
Sugar: 2 g

BASIC BAKED TEMPEH PATTIES

Tempeh patties make great veggie burgers! There are tons of tempeh varieties available, from seven-grain to spicy and even bacon-flavored. Think of tempeh as an adventure; after all, it originally came all the way from Indonesia. Serve on whole-wheat rolls with lettuce and tomato. Mmm, mmm.

SERVES 4

1 (8-ounce) package tempeh, cut into 4 square patties

1 cup plus 2 tablespoons vegetable broth, divided

3 tablespoons soy sauce

2 tablespoons apple cider vinegar

3 cloves garlic, peeled and minced

2 teaspoons sesame oil

1. In a medium saucepan over medium-low heat, simmer tempeh in 1 cup broth for 10 minutes. Drain.
2. Whisk together remaining ingredients, including remaining 2 tablespoons broth. Let tempeh marinate for 3 hours.
3. Preheat oven to 375°F.
4. Cook tempeh on a baking sheet greased with vegan margarine for 12 minutes on each side. *Finito!*

Per Serving:
Calories: 138
Fat: 9 g
Protein: 12 g

Sodium: 265 mg
Fiber: 0 g
Carbohydrates: 6 g
Sugar: 0 g

INTERNATIONAL MAIN DISHES

FOR YOUR ADVENTUROUS SIDE

CARIBBEAN

CUBAN BLACK BEANS, SWEET POTATOES, AND RICE

One great thing about rice is that it lends itself perfectly to citrus flavors and sweetness. You can have a filling meal with a twist: lime, lemon, or even tangerine. Enjoy this dish as a meal or a side, and serve alongside some orange slices, melon, or spicy seasoned tempeh.

SERVES 4

- 3 cloves garlic, peeled and minced
- ½ medium white onion, peeled and chopped
- 2 tablespoons olive oil
- 3 large sweet potatoes, peeled and chopped small
- 2 (15-ounce) cans black beans, drained
- ¼ cup vegetable broth
- 2 cups cooked brown rice
- 1 tablespoon chili powder
- 1 teaspoon paprika
- 1 teaspoon ground cumin
- 1 tablespoon lime juice
- ½ teaspoon hot sauce

1. In a large pot over medium-high heat, sauté garlic and onion in oil for about 3 minutes.
2. Lower the heat to medium-low. Add remaining ingredients except lime juice and hot sauce. Simmer, covered, for 25 minutes.
3. Add lime juice and hot sauce to the pot, and serve while still warm and steamy.

Per Serving:
Calories: 481
Fat: 9 g
Protein: 18 g

Sodium: 510 mg
Fiber: 19 g
Carbohydrates: 84 g
Sugar: 6 g

CARIBBEAN RED BEANS AND RICE

A complete classic. If you have it around, toss in some vegan bacon or ham.

SERVES 4

3 cloves garlic, peeled and crushed

1 small yellow onion, peeled and chopped

2 tablespoons olive oil

2 tablespoons chopped fresh Italian flat-leaf parsley

½ teaspoon dried rosemary leaves

½ teaspoon dried thyme leaves

¼ teaspoon ground cloves

1 (15-ounce) can kidney beans, drained

3 cups vegetable broth

2 bay leaves

1½ cups white rice

⅛ teaspoon salt

⅛ teaspoon ground black pepper

1. In a large saucepan over medium-high heat, sauté garlic and onion in oil for about 3 minutes until soft. Add parsley, rosemary, thyme, and cloves, and continue cooking while mixing in.

2. Add beans, stirring until coated in oil. Cook for about 2 minutes, stirring continually. Add remaining ingredients except salt and pepper. Reduce heat to low, cover, and cook for 30 minutes.

3. Uncover, and let cook for another 10 minutes until liquid is absorbed. Season with salt and pepper. Remember to take out the bay leaves before eating.

PART-TIME TIP

Cooking with dried beans is often much less expensive than canned. It also allows you to control how much sodium you get in your serving of legumes, while canned beans are often surreptitiously filled with salt. Approximately ⅔ cup dried beans equals 1 (15-ounce) can of beans.

Per Serving:
Calories: 441
Fat: 8 g
Protein: 12 g

Sodium: 1,530 mg
Fiber: 5 g
Carbohydrates: 79 g
Sugar: 5 g

TROPICAL COUSCOUS

Sweet—and full of island flavor. The chopped almonds provide a satisfying crunch, and the sliced fresh melon makes a cool addition to the dish. If you're really in a tropical mindset, drink a fresh papaya smoothie. And if you get the urge to begin a hula dance while taking your first bite, by all means go for it.

SERVES 2

1 cup unsweetened coconut milk

1 cup pineapple juice

1 cup couscous

½ teaspoon vanilla extract

2 tablespoons light agave nectar

¼ cup chopped raw almonds

½ cup sliced honeydew melon

1. In a medium saucepan over low heat, bring milk and pineapple juice to a simmer (liquid should be moving, but no bubbles should be forming). Don't boil!

2. Add couscous and let cook for 1 minute. Add vanilla. Shut the heat off, letting everything sit for 5 minutes.

3. Stir in agave nectar, almonds, and melon.

THE SKINNY ON...AGAVE NECTAR

Agave nectar comes in two varieties: light and amber. Like maple syrup grades A or B, agave flavor varies from intense to mild. Amber agave has a stronger flavor, whereas light agave simply tastes more like generic sugar.

Per Serving:
Calories: 561
Fat: 9 g
Protein: 15 g

Sodium: 27 mg
Fiber: 6 g
Carbohydrates: 106 g
Sugar: 33 g

PINEAPPLE-GLAZED TOFU

A great dish for hot weather days. Serve with a little rice and a light green salad. You'll soon be cool as a cucumber—or rather, a pineapple.

SERVES 3

$1/2$ cup pineapple preserves

2 tablespoons balsamic vinegar

2 tablespoons soy sauce

$2/3$ cup pineapple juice

1 (1-pound) block extra-firm tofu, cubed

2 tablespoons white whole-wheat flour

2 tablespoons coconut oil

1 tablespoon cornstarch

1. Whisk preserves, vinegar, soy sauce, and pineapple juice together in a small bowl.
2. Coat tofu with flour on both sides.
3. In a medium saucepan over medium heat, sauté tofu in oil for 2 minutes until golden. Turn the heat down to medium-low, and add pineapple sauce mixture. Stir.
4. Cook for 4 minutes, then add cornstarch. Whisk to avoid lumps. Allow sauce to thicken up for 3 minutes and aloha, you're done.

Per Serving:
Calories: 451
Fat: 17 g
Protein: 18 g

Sodium: 697 mg
Fiber: 3 g
Carbohydrates: 56 g
Sugar: 34 g

MEDITERRANEAN

BLACK BEAN POLENTA CAKES WITH SALSA

All the flavors of the Southwest combine in this colorful confetti polenta loaf. Pan fry individual slices, if you like, or just enjoy it as it is.

SERVES 4

1 (15-ounce) can black beans, drained

6 cups water

2 cups cornmeal

½ medium red bell pepper, seeded and diced small

¾ teaspoon ground cumin

1 teaspoon chili powder

1 teaspoon garlic powder

¾ teaspoon dried oregano leaves

½ teaspoon salt

½ teaspoon ground black pepper

2 tablespoons vegan margarine

¾ cup organic salsa

1. Place black beans in a bowl and mash with a fork until halfway mashed. Set aside.

2. Bring the water to a boil, then slowly add cornmeal, stirring to combine.

3. Reduce heat to low, and cook for 10 minutes, stirring frequently and scraping the bottom of the pot to prevent sticking and burning.

4. Add diced bell pepper, cumin, chili powder, garlic powder, oregano, salt, and pepper and stir well to combine. Continue to heat, stirring frequently for 8–10 more minutes.

5. Add vegan margarine and stir well to combine, then add black beans, combining well.

6. Gently press into a lightly greased loaf pan, smoothing the top with the back of a spoon. Chill until firm, at least 1 hour. Reheat, slice, and serve topped with salsa.

Per Serving:
Calories: 365
Fat: 8 g
Protein: 10 g

Sodium: 567 mg
Fiber: 16 g
Carbohydrates: 64 g
Sugar: 1 g

GREEK LEMON RICE WITH SPINACH

A light, zesty recipe, reminiscent of the Greek dish *spanakorizo*. Go on, fair Hestia, impress me.

SERVES 4

- 1 medium yellow onion, peeled and chopped
- 4 cloves garlic, peeled and minced
- 2 tablespoons olive oil
- ¾ cup white rice
- 2½ cups vegetable broth
- 1 (8-ounce) can tomato paste
- 2 bunches fresh spinach, trimmed
- 2 tablespoons chopped fresh Italian flat-leaf parsley
- 1 tablespoon chopped fresh mint
- 2 tablespoons lemon juice
- ½ teaspoon salt
- ½ teaspoon ground black pepper

1. In a large skillet over medium-high heat, sauté onion and garlic in oil for about 3 minutes. Add rice and brown lightly, making certain to stir occasionally, for about 2 minutes.

2. Add broth, cover, and cook for 12 minutes. Add tomato paste, spinach, and parsley, re-cover, and cook for 5 more minutes.

3. Stir in all remaining ingredients. Remove from heat and serve warm!

Per Serving:
Calories: 163
Fat: 8 g
Protein: 6 g

Sodium: 800 mg
Fiber: 5 g
Carbohydrates: 21 g
Sugar: 4 g

SPANISH ARTICHOKE AND ZUCCHINI PAELLA

What is paella, you ask? It's a traditional Spanish rice dish, served as a main course, that originated in the province of Valencia. This take on the beloved favorite has turmeric in it rather than saffron (because that stuff is expensive!).

SERVES 4

- 3 cloves garlic, peeled and minced
- 1 medium yellow onion, peeled and minced
- 2 tablespoons olive oil
- 1 cup white rice
- 1 (15-ounce) can crushed tomatoes, undrained
- 1 medium green bell pepper, seeded and chopped
- 1 medium red bell pepper, seeded and chopped
- ½ cup chopped canned artichoke hearts, drained
- 2 medium zucchini, sliced
- 2 cups vegetable broth
- 1 tablespoon paprika
- ½ teaspoon ground turmeric
- ¼ teaspoon chopped fresh Italian flat-leaf parsley
- ½ teaspoon salt

1. In a large skillet over medium-high heat, cook garlic and onion in oil for about 4 minutes. Add rice and heat for 1 minute, making sure to constantly stir so that nothing sticks or burns.
2. Add remaining ingredients, stirring to get everything mixed in evenly. Reduce heat to low, cover, and let simmer for 20 minutes.

THE SKINNY ON...GARLIC

Did you know garlic is known to have antiviral and antibacterial properties? Garlic contains an amino acid called allicin. When consumed raw, allicin breaks up biosynthesis in the formation of cell walls, helping to destroy harmful bacteria. Consuming fresh garlic can be good for your health! Pretty cool.

Per Serving:
Calories: 349
Fat: 8 g
Protein: 9 g

Sodium: 893 mg
Fiber: 6 g
Carbohydrates: 62 g
Sugar: 11 g

MEDITERRANEAN QUINOA PILAF

You don't need to spend a fortune to experience the rich, lively flavors of the Mediterranean coast. Pop open a bottle of red wine and pass it around with this dish. Remember to share with the whole family in true Italian style.

SERVES 4

1½ cups quinoa

3 cups vegetable broth

3 tablespoons balsamic vinegar

1 tablespoon lemon juice

2 tablespoons olive oil

⅓ teaspoon salt

½ cup sun-dried tomatoes, chopped

½ cup canned artichoke hearts, drained

½ cup sliced Kalamata olives

1. In a large stockpot over high heat, add quinoa and broth. Bring to a boil, and then lower to a simmer on low heat. Continue cooking, covered, for 20 minutes, until quinoa is cooked through and liquid is evaporated.

2. Add vinegar, lemon juice, oil, and salt, and fluff with a fork. Allow to sit for 1 minute, then add remaining ingredients, stirring well.

PART-TIME TIP

Have some other Italian ingredients lying around? Toss in some chopped fresh tomatoes or chopped fresh parsley. Add some pepperoncini and red onion for an extra kick!

Per Serving:
Calories: 396
Fat: 17 g
Protein: 11 g

Sodium: 1,052 mg
Fiber: 5 g
Carbohydrates: 51 g
Sugar: 4 g

BULGUR WHEAT TABBOULEH SALAD WITH TOMATOES

A traditional Mediterranean dish that is juicy and full of the taste of fresh parsley and mint. This is great alongside hummus and falafel.

SERVES 4

1¼ cups vegetable broth

1 cup bulgur wheat

3 tablespoons olive oil

¼ cup lemon juice

1 teaspoon garlic powder

½ teaspoon sea salt

½ teaspoon ground black pepper

3 scallions, chopped

½ cup chopped fresh mint

½ cup chopped fresh Italian flat-leaf parsley

3 large tomatoes, chopped

1. In a small saucepan over high heat, bring broth to a boil.
2. Place bulgur in a medium bowl. Pour boiling broth over bulgur. Cover and let sit for 30 minutes.
3. Toss bulgur with oil, lemon juice, garlic powder, and salt. Add remaining ingredients and fluff mixture with a fork, adding tomatoes at the end.
4. Chill covered for 1 hour, and serve.

Per Serving:
Calories: 255
Fat: 11 g
Protein: 7 g

Sodium: 517 mg
Fiber: 7 g
Carbohydrates: 37 g
Sugar: 5 g

LEMON BASIL TOFU

Tart and zesty. This chewy tofu dish tastes great over angel hair pasta with a little vegan margarine and nutritional yeast. And throw some white wine in there too. (You deserve it!)

SERVES 6

3 tablespoons lemon juice

1 tablespoon soy sauce

2 teaspoons apple cider vinegar

1 tablespoon Dijon mustard

¾ teaspoon granulated sugar

3 tablespoons olive oil

2 tablespoons chopped fresh basil

2 (1-pound) blocks extra-firm tofu, pressed and sliced into ½"-thick pieces

1. Whisk all ingredients except tofu together in a large bowl.
2. Place tofu in marinade, cover tightly, and let sit in the refrigerator for 3 hours.
3. Preheat oven to 350°F.
4. Cook tofu for 15 minutes on a baking sheet greased with vegan margarine, and then turn over. Cook for another 12 minutes, and eat!

Per Serving:
Calories: 216
Fat: 15 g
Protein: 16 g

Sodium: 234 mg
Fiber: 2 g
Carbohydrates: 5 g
Sugar: 1 g

GREEK SEITAN GYRO

You can now make this delicious street food specialty right in your kitchen. Enjoy with pita chips and hummus, or grape leaves and tabbouleh salad. Go Greek for a day. Lounge around naked and pretend you're a god. Just don't walk around the neighborhood.

SERVES 6

¾ teaspoon paprika

½ teaspoon chopped fresh Italian flat-leaf parsley

¼ teaspoon garlic powder

¼ teaspoon dried oregano leaves

⅛ teaspoon salt

⅛ teaspoon ground black pepper

1 (16-ounce) package seitan, thinly sliced

2 tablespoons olive oil

6 whole-wheat pitas

1 medium tomato, sliced thin

1 medium yellow onion, peeled and chopped

½ medium head lettuce, shredded

½ cup nondairy sour cream

1. In a small bowl, mix together paprika, parsley, garlic powder, oregano, salt, and pepper. Coat seitan in spices.

2. In a medium skillet over medium-low heat, sauté seitan in oil for 7 minutes until browned.

3. Top each pita with seitan, tomato, onion, lettuce, and sour cream.

Per Serving:
Calories: 347
Fat: 9 g
Protein: 9 g

Sodium: 697 mg
Fiber: 6 g
Carbohydrates: 48 g
Sugar: 5 g

ITALIAN TOFU LASAGNA

But how can you have lasagna without ricotta? Easy: with a little tofu and nutritional yeast! We promise it is delicious!

SERVES 4

1 (1-pound) firm block tofu

1 (12-ounce) block silken tofu

½ cup nutritional yeast

1 tablespoon lemon juice

1 tablespoon soy sauce

1 teaspoon garlic powder

2 teaspoons dried basil leaves

3 tablespoons chopped fresh Italian flat-leaf parsley

1 teaspoon salt

4 cups spaghetti sauce

1 (16-ounce) package lasagna noodles, cooked

1 (8-ounce) package shredded mozzarella-flavored vegan cheese

1. Preheat oven to 350°F.
2. In a medium bowl, mash together tofus, nutritional yeast, lemon juice, soy sauce, garlic powder, basil, parsley, and salt until completely ground into a ricotta consistency.
3. Layer the bottom of an ungreased 9" × 13" casserole dish with a portion of sauce. Add a layer of noodles, followed by a layer of tofu mixture. Continue layering until everything is used up!
4. Sprinkle top of lasagna with cheese. Cover with aluminum foil, and bake for 25 minutes. Try not to build the lasagna over the top of the casserole pan—you don't want any explosions.

Per Serving:
Calories: 909
Fat: 27 g
Protein: 38 g

Sodium: 2,499 mg
Fiber: 15 g
Carbohydrates: 126 g
Sugar: 16 g

BELLISSIMO ITALIAN RICE SALAD

The flavors of Italy are decadent and rich. The sweet smell of tomato sauce and the savory flavors of cheese recall the romantic serenade of the accordion over dinner by candlelight. Luckily you can recreate these taste memories in a very vegan way.

SERVES 4

- 1 tablespoon balsamic vinegar
- 1/3 cup red wine vinegar
- 2 teaspoons Dijon mustard
- 4 cloves garlic, peeled and minced
- 1 teaspoon dried basil leaves
- 1/3 cup chopped fresh Italian flat-leaf parsley
- 1/2 cup olive oil
- 2 cups cooked brown rice
- 1 (14-ounce) can diced tomatoes, undrained
- 1 medium carrot, peeled and grated
- 1/2 cup chopped roasted red peppers
- 1/2 cup sliced green olives
- 1/4 cup nutritional yeast
- 1/8 teaspoon salt
- 1/8 teaspoon ground black pepper

1. In a small bowl, whisk together balsamic vinegar, red wine vinegar, mustard, garlic, basil, parsley, and oil.
2. In a large bowl, mix rice and remaining ingredients together. Add vinegar mixture to rice mixture. Stir well.
3. Chill covered in the refrigerator for 30 minutes before serving.

Per Serving:
Calories: 468
Fat: 31 g
Protein: 7 g

Sodium: 870 mg
Fiber: 5 g
Carbohydrates: 40 g
Sugar: 7 g

BREADED EGGPLANT "PARMESAN"

A favorite of vegans and non-vegans alike. The perfect complement to your presentation Italiano. The *pièce de résistance*. The Sistine Chapel of your glorious catalog.

SERVES 4

1 medium eggplant, peeled and cut into ³/₄"-thick slices

¹/₂ teaspoon salt

³/₄ cup white whole-wheat flour

1 teaspoon garlic powder

²/₃ cup unsweetened soy milk

Egg replacement mixture (equivalent of 2 eggs), prepared according to package directions

1¹/₂ cups bread crumbs

2 tablespoons Italian seasoning

¹/₄ cup nutritional yeast

1¹/₂ cups marinara sauce

1 (8-ounce) package shredded mozzarella-flavored vegan cheese

1. On an ungreased baking tray, sprinkle eggplant with salt. Let sit for 10 minutes, then drain excess moisture.
2. Set up 3 small bowls. In the first bowl, mix flour and garlic powder. In the second bowl, whisk up milk and egg replacer. In the third, mix bread crumbs, Italian seasoning, and nutritional yeast.
3. Coat eggplant pieces with flour mixture, then gently dip into milk mixture, and lastly dredge in bread crumb mixture. Place into a 9" × 13" casserole dish greased with vegan margarine.
4. Bake for 25 minutes. Remove from the oven, cover in marinara sauce, and sprinkle on cheese, then bake for another 5 minutes.

Per Serving:
Calories: 476
Fat: 18 g
Protein: 13 g

Sodium: 1,458 mg
Fiber: 13 g
Carbohydrates: 68 g
Sugar: 14 g

ARTICHOKE AND SPINACH PESTO PASTA

The tartness of artichokes and leafy freshness of pesto make this a succulent and filling dish packed with the nutritional benefits of spinach and the good monosaturated fats of walnuts. Super brain food for a super human like you!

SERVES 4

1 cup fresh basil leaves

1 cup fresh spinach leaves

3 cloves garlic, peeled

½ cup raw walnuts

1 tablespoon lemon juice

2 tablespoons nutritional yeast

½ teaspoon salt

½ teaspoon ground black pepper

2 tablespoons olive oil

1 cup chopped canned artichoke hearts, drained

2 tablespoons vegan margarine

1 tablespoon white whole-wheat flour

¾ cup unsweetened soy milk

2 cups cooked whole-wheat pasta

1 medium avocado, peeled, pitted, and diced

1. In a food processor, process basil, spinach, garlic, walnuts, lemon juice, nutritional yeast, salt, and pepper. Stop when mixture is almost smooth. Add oil and artichokes, continuing to process until artichokes are diced very small. Set aside.

2. In a small saucepan, melt margarine for 30 seconds over medium-low heat and add flour, followed by milk. Cook until thick and paste-like.

3. Combine basil mixture with margarine mixture. Toss with pasta and diced avocados. Serve warm.

Per Serving:
Calories: 449
Fat: 32 g
Protein: 12 g

Sodium: 510 mg
Fiber: 8 g
Carbohydrates: 35 g
Sugar: 3 g

EGGPLANT PUTTANESCA

Eggplant holds any flavor well, which works perfectly for tangy puttanesca sauce. Try using this sauce, including the eggplant, on top of pasta or on a pizza crust sans the capers. The intense flavor of capers can be a little too strong for a small slice of pizza.

SERVES 4

2 tablespoons olive oil

1 medium red bell pepper, seeded and chopped

1 medium eggplant, peeled and chopped

3 cloves garlic, peeled and minced

2 tablespoons capers

⅓ cup sliced Kalamata olives

½ teaspoon crushed red pepper flakes

1 (14-ounce) can diced tomatoes, undrained

1 tablespoon balsamic vinegar

½ teaspoon chopped fresh Italian flat-leaf parsley

2 cups cooked pasta

1. In a large saucepan over medium-high heat, heat oil for 30 seconds. Sauté bell pepper and eggplant for 5 minutes. Add garlic and sauté for an additional 2 minutes. Add capers, olives, and red pepper flakes, and stir continuously for about 1 minute.

2. Reduce heat to low, and add tomatoes, vinegar, and parsley. Cover and simmer for 12 minutes. Serve over pasta.

Per Serving:
Calories: 283
Fat: 11 g
Protein: 8 g

Sodium: 467 mg
Fiber: 8 g
Carbohydrates: 41 g
Sugar: 11 g

GNOCCHI AND WALNUT PARSLEY SAUCE

Gnocchi is a delicious, chewy pasta made from potatoes. Being a root earth vegetable, potato pairs well with rich and savory sauces. Here walnuts lend a smooth and maple-like flavor, while parsley adds some herbal high notes. It sounds like a symphony! Of food! How marvelous.

SERVES 4

1 cup chopped raw walnuts

2½ cups unsweetened soy milk

2 tablespoons vegan margarine

2 tablespoons white whole-wheat flour

½ teaspoon chopped fresh Italian flat-leaf parsley

2 teaspoons nutritional yeast

½ teaspoon salt

¼ teaspoon ground black pepper

1 (17.5-ounce) package vegan gnocchi, cooked

1. In a large saucepan over low heat, cook walnuts in milk for approximately 5 minutes to soften. Remove from heat and set aside.

2. In another large saucepan, heat margarine and flour over medium-low heat for 1 minute. Stir constantly. Very slowly, whisk in walnut mixture. Stir continuously for about 5 minutes until sauce thickens.

3. Remove from heat. Add in parsley, nutritional yeast, salt, and pepper. Serve over cooked gnocchi.

PART-TIME TIP

When cooking with any nondairy milk, it's always best to stick to unsweetened varieties when you're not making dessert. You don't want your pasta sauce to taste like vanilla and sugar, do you?

Per Serving:
Calories: 602
Fat: 29 g
Protein: 18 g

Sodium: 1,042 mg
Fiber: 7 g
Carbohydrates: 70 g
Sugar: 8 g

CREAMY SUN-DRIED TOMATO PASTA

A sweet and rich sauce that happens to be low in fat. How'd that happen? It's vegan, that's how.

SERVES 6

1 (1-pound) block silken tofu, well pressed

¼ cup unsweetened soy milk

2 tablespoons red wine vinegar

½ teaspoon jarred minced garlic

½ teaspoon granulated sugar

½ teaspoon salt

1¼ cups sun-dried tomatoes in oil

1 teaspoon dried parsley leaves

1 (12-ounce) package whole-wheat pasta, cooked

2 tablespoons chopped fresh basil

1. Process all ingredients, except pasta and basil, in a food processor until very smooth.
2. Transfer mixture to a large saucepan and heat on low about 10 minutes.
3. Pour mixture over cooked pasta, sprinkle with chopped basil, and dig in!

Per Serving:
Calories: 291
Fat: 6 g
Protein: 13 g

Sodium: 269 mg
Fiber: 6 g
Carbohydrates: 50 g
Sugar: 3 g

TOFU "RICOTTA" MANICOTTI

In vegan cooking, one of your best friends is the quotation mark: "ricotta," "steak," "beef," and so on. Basically, quotations marks here should be synonymous for *awesome*. Enjoy this veganized Tofu Awesome Ricotta Awesome Manicotti.

SERVES 4

- 2 (1-pound) blocks firm tofu, crumbled
- 2 tablespoons lemon juice
- 2 tablespoons olive oil
- 2 tablespoons unsweetened soy milk
- 1/4 cup nutritional yeast
- 1/2 teaspoon garlic powder
- 1/2 teaspoon onion powder
- 1/2 teaspoon salt
- 1 teaspoon dried basil leaves
- 2 tablespoons chopped fresh Italian flat-leaf parsley
- 12 large manicotti, cooked according to package instructions
- 2 cups marinara sauce, divided
- 1/3 cup grated vegan cheese

1. Preheat oven to 350°F.
2. Mash up tofu with lemon juice, oil, milk, nutritional yeast, garlic powder, onion powder, salt, basil, and parsley in a large bowl. Mix well until consistency is almost smooth.
3. Stuff manicotti with tofu mixture.
4. Cover the bottom of a greased 9" × 13" casserole dish with 1 cup marinara sauce and line up manicotti inside. Cover with cheese and remaining sauce. Bake for 30 minutes.

Per Serving:
Calories: 572
Fat: 24 g
Protein: 31 g

Sodium: 1,051 mg
Fiber: 8 g
Carbohydrates: 58 g
Sugar: 9 g

CLASSIC FETTUCCINE ALFREDO

Most vegan Alfredo recipes start with a roux of margarine and soy milk, but this one uses cashew cream instead for a sensually decadent white sauce. Go ahead and lick the spoons; nobody's watching.

SERVES 6

½ cup raw cashews

1¼ cups water

1 tablespoon miso

2 tablespoons lemon juice

2 tablespoons Homemade Tahini (see recipe in Chapter 3)

¼ cup peeled, diced yellow onion

1 teaspoon peeled, minced garlic

½ teaspoon salt

¼ cup nutritional yeast

2 tablespoons olive oil

1 (12-ounce) package fettuccine, cooked

1. Blend together the cashews and water until completely smooth and creamy, about 90 seconds.
2. Add remaining ingredients, except oil and pasta, and purée until smooth. Slowly add oil until thick and oil is emulsified.
3. Heat in a medium saucepan over low heat for 4–5 minutes, stirring frequently. Serve over cooked fettuccine noodles.

Per Serving:
Calories: 358
Fat: 13 g
Protein: 12 g

Sodium: 317 mg
Fiber: 3 g
Carbohydrates: 49 g
Sugar: 4 g

LEMON, BASIL, AND ARTICHOKE PASTA

All of these main ingredients have sharp, bright flavors that will be a treat for your taste buds. Try eating the sauce with bowtie pasta and a side of roasted red potatoes.

SERVES 4

- 1 (12-ounce) package whole-wheat pasta, cooked
- 1 (6-ounce) can artichoke hearts, drained and chopped
- 2 large tomatoes, chopped
- $\frac{1}{2}$ cup chopped fresh basil
- $\frac{1}{2}$ cup sliced black olives
- 2 tablespoons olive oil
- 1 tablespoon lemon juice
- $\frac{1}{2}$ teaspoon dried rosemary leaves
- 2 tablespoons nutritional yeast
- $\frac{1}{8}$ teaspoon salt
- $\frac{1}{8}$ teaspoon ground black pepper

In a large saucepan on low heat, mix pasta with all remaining ingredients. Heat well, stirring continuously, for about 4 minutes. Serve warm.

Per Serving:
Calories: 254
Fat: 12 g
Protein: 8 g
Sodium: 368 mg
Fiber: 5 g
Carbohydrates: 33 g
Sugar: 3 g

ASIAN

SESAME BAKED TOFU

A meaty and deliciously flavorful dish. Serve atop a nice big plate of steamed brown rice with peas and bamboo shoots. You don't need a cookie to know your fortune this time: your guests are going to love it.

SERVES 6

¼ cup soy sauce

2 tablespoons sesame oil

¾ teaspoon garlic powder

½ teaspoon ground ginger

2 (1-pound) blocks extra-firm tofu, well pressed and cut into 1½"-thick slices

4 tablespoons sesame seeds

1. In a small bowl, whisk together soy sauce, oil, garlic powder, and ginger.
2. Place tofu in a large shallow dish. Add marinade. Let sit for at least 1 hour.
3. Preheat oven to 400°F. Coat a baking sheet with olive oil.
4. Bake tofu on sheet for 25 minutes. Turn over and bake for another 10 minutes.
5. Toss tofu in sesame seeds to coat.

Per Serving:
Calories: 232
Fat: 16 g
Protein: 18 g

Sodium: 677 mg
Fiber: 3 g
Carbohydrates: 6 g
Sugar: 1 g

ASIAN SESAME NOODLES

Use any kind of pasta you have lying around if you can't make it to the store. Tangy and tasty, here is your fortune: you'll get addicted to this easy-to-make sauce.

SERVES 4

½ cup Homemade Tahini (see recipe in Chapter 3)

½ cup water

2 tablespoons soy sauce

1 clove garlic, peeled

2 teaspoons fresh minced ginger

2 tablespoons rice vinegar

1 medium red bell pepper, seeded and sliced very thin

2 scallions, chopped

¾ cup chopped fresh snow peas

2 teaspoons sesame oil

1 (1-pound) package udon noodles, cooked according to package instructions

¼ teaspoon crushed red pepper flakes

1. In a blender, combine tahini, water, soy sauce, garlic, ginger, and vinegar.
2. In a large saucepan over medium-high heat, sauté bell pepper, scallions, and snow peas in oil for 3 minutes. Add tahini mixture and noodles, stirring until completely combined.
3. Cook for 4 more minutes. Garnish with crushed red pepper flakes and serve!

Per Serving:
Calories: 623
Fat: 23 g
Protein: 16 g

Sodium: 892 mg
Fiber: 6 g
Carbohydrates: 90 g
Sugar: 2 g

SWEET AND SOUR TEMPEH

The enigmatic flavor will leave you both puzzled and pleased. Try some hearty brown rice with this dish to mix with the sauce.

SERVES 4

1 cup vegetable broth

2 tablespoons soy sauce

1 (8-ounce) package tempeh, diced

2 tablespoons barbecue sauce

2 teaspoons maple syrup

½ teaspoon ground ginger

⅓ cup apple cider vinegar

1 tablespoon cornstarch

1 (15-ounce) can pineapple chunks, divided into chunks and juice

2 tablespoons olive oil

1 medium yellow bell pepper, seeded and chopped

1 medium red bell pepper, seeded and chopped

1 medium yellow onion, peeled and chopped

1. Whisk broth and soy sauce in a medium saucepan. Set on stove over low heat, and simmer 5 minutes. Add tempeh and continue simmering for 10 minutes.
2. Remove tempeh and strain, reserving ½ cup broth.
3. Whisk barbecue sauce, syrup, ginger, vinegar, cornstarch, and pineapple juice in a small bowl. Make sure no clumps remain.
4. In a medium skillet over medium heat, heat oil for 30 seconds, then toast tempeh, bell peppers, and onion for 2 minutes.
5. Add sauce mixture to skillet and allow to simmer, cooking for 8 minutes until thickened. Top with pineapple chunks.

Per Serving:
Calories: 297
Fat: 13 g
Protein: 14 g

Sodium: 766 mg
Fiber: 2 g
Carbohydrates: 32 g
Sugar: 20 g

CHINESE FRIED RICE WITH TOFU AND CASHEWS

Chinese food is incredible for its mastery of mixing both savory and sweet flavors. This recipe takes plain old boiled white rice (which you can make and store all week) and turns it into something delicious.

SERVES 3

2 cloves garlic, peeled and minced

1 (12-ounce) block tofu, cut into ½"-thick cubes

3 tablespoons olive oil, divided

3 cups cooked white rice

½ cup frozen mixed vegetables

3 tablespoons soy sauce

1 tablespoon sesame oil

¼ teaspoon granulated sugar

¼ cup all-natural peanut butter

2 tablespoons lime juice

3 scallions, diced

⅓ cup chopped raw cashews

1. In a large skillet over medium-high heat, sauté garlic and tofu in 2 tablespoons olive oil for about 8 minutes until tofu is browned.

2. Add rice, vegetables, and remaining olive oil. Stir well. Add soy sauce, sesame oil, sugar, and peanut butter. Stir constantly, allowing everything to cook for 4 minutes.

3. Remove from heat, and add lime juice, scallions, and cashews.

Per Serving:
Calories: 788
Fat: 47 g
Protein: 28 g

Sodium: 1,030 mg
Fiber: 6 g
Carbohydrates: 69 g
Sugar: 7 g

SAUCY KUNG PAO TOFU

This dish packs a wallop and a *POW!* (If this dish were a comic book page, you would have just been knocked out by big yellow text!) Cook the tofu with some bamboo shoots, Asian noodles, or snap peas and carrots.

SERVES 6

3 tablespoons soy sauce

2 tablespoons rice vinegar

1 tablespoon sesame oil

2 (1-pound) blocks firm tofu, chopped

1 medium red bell pepper, seeded and chopped

$2/3$ cup sliced white mushrooms

3 cloves garlic, peeled

2 small red chilies, seeded and diced

1 teaspoon crushed red pepper flakes

2 tablespoons olive oil

1 teaspoon ground ginger

$1/2$ cup vegetable broth

$1/2$ teaspoon granulated sugar

$1^1/2$ teaspoons cornstarch

2 scallions, chopped

$1/2$ cup raw peanuts

1. In a small bowl, whisk together soy sauce, vinegar, and sesame oil. Pour into a shallow dish. Add tofu and let marinate for 1 hour. Drain and reserve marinade when finished.

2. In a large saucepan over medium-high heat, sauté bell pepper, mushrooms, garlic, chilies, and red pepper flakes in olive oil for 3 minutes. Add tofu and cook for another 2 minutes until vegetables have become soft and brightly colored.

3. Lower the heat to medium, and add reserved marinade, ginger, broth, sugar, and cornstarch. Be sure to whisk mixture so cornstarch doesn't become lumpy. Stir consistently and let sauce thicken, about 10 minutes.

4. Lastly, add scallions and peanuts, heating for 1 minute. *POW!*

Per Serving:
Calories: 282
Fat: 20 g
Protein: 18 g

Sodium: 569 mg
Fiber: 3 g
Carbohydrates: 10 g
Sugar: 3 g

ORANGE-GLAZED "CHICKEN" TOFU

In the style of your favorite Chinese takeout restaurant, we present to you orange "chicken." Eat it with a side of rice and steamed veggies to complete that lazy evening feel.

SERVES 3

- 2 tablespoons soy sauce
- ²/₃ cup no-pulp orange juice
- 2 tablespoons rice vinegar
- 1 tablespoon maple syrup
- ½ teaspoon crushed red pepper flakes
- 1 (1-pound) block firm tofu, well pressed and chopped
- 3 cloves garlic, peeled and minced
- 2 tablespoons olive oil
- 1½ teaspoons cornstarch
- 2 tablespoons water

1. In a small bowl, whisk up soy sauce, orange juice, vinegar, syrup, and red pepper flakes.

2. In a medium saucepan over medium heat, sauté tofu and garlic in oil for 2 minutes until tofu is lightly browned.

3. Lower heat to medium-low and add orange juice mixture. Bring to a simmer slowly (liquid should be moving, but no bubbles should be forming), and cook for 8 more minutes.

4. Whisk together cornstarch and water in another small bowl. Keep stirring until starch is dissolved—sometimes it can be pesky. Add starch mixture to tofu mixture.

5. Allow to come to a simmer once more (liquid should be moving, but no bubbles should be forming), and cook for 4 minutes.

Per Serving:
Calories: 266
Fat: 16 g
Protein: 15 g

Sodium: 679 mg
Fiber: 2 g
Carbohydrates: 17 g
Sugar: 9 g

UDON NOODLE BUDDHA BOWL

This soup, full of chewy udon noodles, is yummy as an appetizer and cooks in a snap.

SERVES 4

2 (8-ounce) packages udon noodles, cooked and drained

3½ cups Shiitake and Garlic Broth (see recipe in Chapter 5)

1½ teaspoons fresh minced ginger

1 tablespoon granulated sugar

1 tablespoon soy sauce

1 tablespoon rice vinegar

¼ teaspoon crushed red pepper flakes

1 medium head baby bok choy, chopped

1 cup chopped shiitake mushrooms

1 (1-pound) block silken tofu, cubed

¼ cup bean sprouts

1 cup fresh spinach

1 teaspoon sesame oil

1. Place equal amounts cooked noodles into four serving bowls...or one.
2. In a large pot over medium heat, combine Shiitake and Garlic Broth, ginger, sugar, soy sauce, vinegar, and red pepper flakes. Bring broth to a simmer (liquid should be moving, but no bubbles should be forming), and add baby bok choy, mushrooms, and tofu. Let cook for 10 minutes.
3. Add bean sprouts and spinach to the pot, and continue to simmer for 1 minute. Remove from heat, drizzle with oil, and divide into the serving bowls.

Per Serving:
Calories: 528
Fat: 7 g
Protein: 21 g

Sodium: 746 mg
Fiber: 6 g
Carbohydrates: 99 g
Sugar: 8 g

STICKY TERIYAKI TOFU CUBES

What do you do with Sticky Teriyaki Tofu Cubes? First, be prepared to be blown away by how great these taste. Next, toss them in a salad, or eat them as a snack at work. The world is your vegan oyster—do as your heart desires.

SERVES 3

1/3 cup soy sauce

3 tablespoons barbecue sauce

2 teaspoons hot chili sauce

1/4 cup maple syrup

3/4 teaspoon garlic powder

1 (1-pound) block extra-firm tofu, cut into thin chunks

1. Preheat oven to 375°F.
2. In an ungreased 9" × 13" casserole dish, whisk together all ingredients except tofu.
3. Add tofu and stir to make sure it is well covered. Bake for 40 minutes, tossing once halfway through baking.

Per Serving:
Calories: 269
Fat: 8 g
Protein: 19 g

Sodium: 1,973 mg
Fiber: 2 g
Carbohydrates: 31 g
Sugar: 23 g

SWEET AND SPICY PEANUT NOODLES

Such a delicious, dual-natured recipe. Deceptively sweet and then bitingly spicy. The mixture of peanut butter and sesame oil gives this recipe such an exotic flavor, so you'll be revisiting Asia again and again.

SERVES 4

⅓ cup all-natural chunky peanut butter

3 tablespoons soy sauce

⅔ cup pineapple juice

2 cloves garlic, peeled and minced

1 teaspoon ground ginger

½ teaspoon salt

3 small chilies, seeded and minced

⅔ cup diced canned pineapple, drained

1 tablespoon olive oil

1 teaspoon sesame oil

1 (12-ounce) package udon noodles, cooked according to package instructions

1. In a medium saucepan over low heat, cook peanut butter, soy sauce, pineapple juice, garlic, ginger, and salt about 10 minutes. Stir until everything is combined.

2. In a large saucepan over medium heat, cook chilies and pineapple in olive oil and sesame oil until pineapple has browned a bit. Add noodles and stir frequently for about 2 minutes.

3. Reduce heat to low and add peanut sauce, stirring everything together and cooking for another 2 minutes.

Per Serving:
Calories: 506
Fat: 17 g
Protein: 15 g

Sodium: 1,306 mg
Fiber: 4 g
Carbohydrates: 77 g
Sugar: 11 g

CHILI AND CURRY BAKED TOFU

For those with a romantic attachment to spice, a delivery from Yours Truly. Enjoy the Indian-Thai fusion flavors of this dish. Serve with rice or some lentils and vegan naan.

SERVES 3

- ⅓ cup unsweetened coconut milk
- 2 tablespoons maple syrup
- 3 small chilies, seeded and minced
- ½ teaspoon garlic powder
- 1 teaspoon ground cumin
- 1 teaspoon curry powder
- ½ teaspoon ground turmeric
- 1 (1-pound) block extra-firm tofu, sliced thin

1. In a small bowl, whisk up milk, syrup, chilies, garlic powder, cumin, curry powder, and turmeric. Pour into a large shallow dish. Toss in tofu and let marinate for 1 hour.
2. Preheat oven to 425°F.
3. Transfer tofu to an ungreased 9" × 13" casserole dish. Pour 3 teaspoons marinade over tofu, and reserve remaining marinade. Bake for 10 minutes, then turn over and bake for another 10 minutes.
4. Serve with remaining sauce for dipping.

Per Serving:
Calories: 198
Fat: 9 g
Protein: 16 g

Sodium: 12 mg
Fiber: 3 g
Carbohydrates: 15 g
Sugar: 9 g

ORANGE AND RAISIN CURRIED COUSCOUS

Lots of whole grains taste fabulous when morphed from savory to sweet. This pilaf brings the bright sweet notes of orange and combines them with the punch of coriander and curry. A spicy-sweet mix perfect served warm. Try baking up a raisin bread version of traditional naan to enhance the warm flavors.

SERVES 4

2 cups water

1½ cups couscous

½ cup no-pulp orange juice

1 medium yellow onion, peeled and chopped

2 tablespoons extra-virgin olive oil

½ teaspoon ground coriander

½ teaspoon curry powder

3 dates, pitted and chopped

¾ cup golden raisins

¾ cup sliced raw almonds

2 scallions, chopped

1. In a large saucepan, bring water to a boil and add couscous. Remove from heat, stir in orange juice, cover, and allow to sit for 15 minutes.

2. In a small skillet over medium-high heat, sauté onion in oil for about 3 minutes. Add coriander, curry powder, and dates. Cook for another 1 minute. Remove from heat and add mixture to couscous, mixing well.

3. Top with raisins, almonds, and scallions. Serve!

Per Serving:
Calories: 728
Fat: 33 g
Protein: 19 g

Sodium: 14 mg
Fiber: 10 g
Carbohydrates: 95 g
Sugar: 30 g

SPICY CHILI BASIL TOFU

A popular dish in Thailand that is most frequently made with fish. Obviously there's nothing fishy about this recipe—only tofushy.

SERVES 3

4 cloves garlic, peeled and minced

5 small red chilies, seeded and diced

3 medium shallots, diced

2 tablespoons sesame oil

1 (1-pound) block firm tofu, diced

1 tablespoon vegan oyster sauce

1 teaspoon granulated sugar

¼ cup soy sauce

1 bunch fresh Thai basil

1. In a large saucepan over medium heat, cook garlic, chilies, and shallots in oil for 4 minutes until shallots are browned.
2. Add tofu and cook for 3 minutes until tofu is browned.
3. Lower the heat to medium-low. Add oyster sauce, sugar, and soy sauce. Mix well to dissolve sugar. Cook for 4 minutes, then stir in basil, allowing it to wilt for about 3 minutes.

Per Serving:
Calories: 271
Fat: 16 g
Protein: 18 g

Sodium: 1,518 mg
Fiber: 3 g
Carbohydrates: 16 g
Sugar: 6 g

INDIAN TOFU PALAK

A typical palak paneer is a dish of cheese and creamed spinach. Of course, here you'll use tofu—the Magical White Block of Wonder.

SERVES 4

3 cloves garlic, peeled and minced

1 (1-pound) block extra-firm tofu, cubed

2 tablespoons olive oil

2 tablespoons nutritional yeast

½ teaspoon onion powder

4 bunches fresh spinach

3 tablespoons water

1 tablespoon curry powder

2 teaspoons ground cumin

½ teaspoon salt

½ cup plain soy yogurt

1. In a medium saucepan on low heat, sauté garlic and tofu for 1 minute in oil. Add nutritional yeast and onion powder, stirring to coat tofu. Cook for 3 minutes until tofu is browned.
2. Add spinach, water, curry powder, cumin, and salt. As spinach wilts, add yogurt and heat until spinach is soft. This will take about only 1 minute. Enjoy!

Per Serving: Sodium: 489 mg
Calories: 271   Fiber: 9 g
Fat: 14 g   Carbohydrates: 18 g
Protein: 22 g   Sugar: 3 g

TANDOORI SEITAN

A classic Indian dish with a vegan twist. Full of such bright and spicy flavors, one bite might make you break out into song like a Bollywood star! Serve with warm rice.

SERVES 6

- ⅔ cup plain soy yogurt
- 2 tablespoons lemon juice
- 1½ tablespoons tandoori spice blend
- ½ teaspoon ground cumin
- ½ teaspoon garlic powder
- ¼ teaspoon salt
- 1 (16-ounce) package seitan, chopped
- 1 medium yellow onion, peeled and chopped
- 1 medium yellow bell pepper, seeded and chopped
- 1 medium tomato, chopped
- 2 tablespoons olive oil

1. Whisk together yogurt, lemon juice, and all spices in a large bowl. Add in seitan and let marinate for 1 hour. Drain seitan and reserve remaining marinade.
2. In a large skillet over medium-high heat, sauté onion, bell pepper, and tomato in oil for 2 minutes. Reduce heat to low and add seitan. Cook for 10 minutes, tossing every few minutes.
3. Top with remaining marinade and serve.

Per Serving:
Calories: 160
Fat: 5 g
Protein: 15 g

Sodium: 329 mg
Fiber: 2 g
Carbohydrates: 14 g
Sugar: 5 g

MASSAMAN CURRIED SEITAN

A popular dish in Muslim countries, Thailand, and India. It's nice to try something a little different now and then. Unless, of course, you are Muslim, Thai, or Indian. In which case, by all means...carry on.

SERVES 4

1 tablespoon Chinese five-spice powder

½ teaspoon ground ginger

½ teaspoon ground turmeric

¼ teaspoon cayenne pepper

1 tablespoon sesame oil

1 cup vegetable broth

1½ cups unsweetened coconut milk

2 medium red potatoes, peeled and chopped

1½ cups chopped seitan

2 whole cloves

1 teaspoon salt

1 tablespoon all-natural peanut butter

½ teaspoon ground cinnamon

2 teaspoons light brown sugar

⅓ cup raw cashews

1. In a large stockpot over medium heat, combine five-spice powder, ginger, turmeric, and cayenne pepper in oil. Stir continuously for 1 minute.

2. Reduce heat to medium-low, and add broth and milk. Then add potatoes, seitan, cloves, and salt. Cover and cook for 20 minutes, stirring every so often.

3. Uncover, remove cloves, and add peanut butter, cinnamon, brown sugar, and cashews. Cook for 1 minute, and serve warm!

Per Serving:
Calories: 361
Fat: 15 g
Protein: 24 g

Sodium: 1,176 mg
Fiber: 4 g
Carbohydrates: 37 g
Sugar: 8 g

CURRIED RICE AND LENTILS

This recipe is delicious with a little tempeh thrown in. Try adding some chickpeas for extra protein and sopping up scoops of it with whole-wheat vegan naan.

SERVES 4

1½ cups cooked brown rice

1 cup dry red lentils

3½ cups vegetable broth

1 bay leaf

1 tablespoon curry powder

½ teaspoon ground cumin

½ teaspoon ground turmeric

½ teaspoon garlic powder

⅛ teaspoon salt

⅛ teaspoon ground black pepper

1. Combine all the ingredients except salt and pepper in a large pot over medium-high heat. Simmer, covered, for 20 minutes.
2. Season with salt and pepper, and serve.

THE SKINNY ON...NAAN

Naan is a traditional Indian bread. Fluffy and light, it is served warm and is a staple for most Indian dinners. Traditional naan is usually made with milk and butter as well as egg. Luckily you can substitute any naan recipe, ingredient for ingredient, with soy milk, vegan margarine, and egg replacer!

Per Serving:
Calories: 272
Fat: 2 g
Protein: 15 g

Sodium: 652 mg
Fiber: 13 g
Carbohydrates: 51 g
Sugar: 4 g

SIMMERED COCONUT CURRIED TOFU

This dish can be served atop any tropical-flavored rice or even as a toothpick appetizer alongside mango salsa and chips.

SERVES 3

1 (1-pound) block extra-firm tofu, cubed

1 tablespoon olive oil

2 teaspoons sesame oil

3 tablespoons all-natural peanut butter

2 tablespoons soy sauce

2 tablespoons water

1 teaspoon curry powder

¼ cup coconut flakes

2 tablespoons chopped fresh cilantro

1. In a large saucepan over medium-high heat, sauté tofu in olive oil for 2 minutes until slightly golden.
2. Lower the heat to medium-low. Add sesame oil, peanut butter, soy sauce, water, and curry powder. Stir well and heat for about 5 minutes.
3. Add coconut and cilantro, and heat for another 1 minute. Eat up!

Per Serving:
Calories: 352
Fat: 27 g
Protein: 21 g

Sodium: 681 mg
Fiber: 4 g
Carbohydrates: 10 g
Sugar: 3 g

MEXICAN/TEX-MEX

MEXICO CITY PROTEIN BOWL

This delicious dish packs a walloping 23 grams of protein per serving. It can also be divided into smaller portions as a side to a main meal.

SERVES 2

½ (1-pound) block silken tofu, diced small

1 scallion, chopped

1 tablespoon olive oil

½ cup frozen peas, thawed

½ cup frozen corn, thawed

½ teaspoon chili powder

1 (15-ounce) can black beans, drained

2 (8") corn tortillas

⅛ teaspoon hot sauce

1. In a large saucepan over medium heat, cook tofu and scallion in oil for 3 minutes. Add peas, corn, and chili powder. Stir frequently, cooking for another 2 minutes.

2. Lower the heat to medium-low, and add beans. Cook for 5 minutes.

3. Spoon mixture onto corn tortillas. (Rest tortillas at the bottom of a medium bowl for this to be a "Protein Bowl.") Season with hot sauce!

Per Serving:
Calories: 466
Fat: 12 g
Protein: 23 g

Sodium: 409 mg
Fiber: 17 g
Carbohydrates: 71 g
Sugar: 5 g

MEXICAN SPICE-CRUSTED TOFU WITH CASHEW SOUR CREAM

It's not Cinco de Mayo, but that doesn't mean you can't celebrate this amazing dish. This is a great rice topper or substitute to use for taco "meat" in corn or lettuce taco shells. Add some black beans, and you've got yourself a satisfying meal.

SERVES 3

MEXICAN SPICE-CRUSTED TOFU

2 tablespoons soy sauce

3 tablespoons hot chili sauce

1 teaspoon granulated sugar

1 (1-pound) block extra-firm tofu, sliced into strips

1 teaspoon garlic powder

1 teaspoon onion powder

1 tablespoon chili powder

$3/4$ teaspoon ground cumin

$3/4$ teaspoon dried oregano leaves

2 tablespoons white whole-wheat flour

CASHEW SOUR CREAM DIPPING SAUCE

$1/2$ cup raw cashews, soaked for 1 hour

$1/2$ cup water

$1 1/2$ tablespoons lemon juice

4 teaspoons apple cider vinegar

1. **TO MAKE MEXICAN SPICE-CRUSTED TOFU:** Preheat oven to 350°F.

2. In a large bowl, whisk soy sauce, chili sauce, and sugar. Add tofu and let marinate for $1 1/2$ hours.

3. Mix remaining ingredients in a separate small bowl. Carefully rub tofu into spice mix on both sides, and place on a baking sheet lightly greased with vegan margarine. Bake for 9 minutes, turning once halfway through baking.

4. **TO MAKE CASHEW SOUR CREAM DIPPING SAUCE:** Process cashews, water, lemon juice, and vinegar in a food processor. Spoon into a small bowl for dipping.

Per Serving:
Calories: 320
Fat: 18 g
Protein: 22 g

Sodium: 764 mg
Fiber: 5 g
Carbohydrates: 20 g
Sugar: 4 g

229

TOFU AND PORTOBELLO "ENCHILADAS"

The tofu will fill you up, and the portobello mushrooms add a sophisticated flavor. Stuff in some vegan cheese and top with a little hot sauce to get the full effect.

SERVES 4

1 (1-pound) block firm tofu, diced small

5 portobello mushrooms, gills removed and chopped

1 medium yellow onion, peeled and diced

3 cloves garlic, peeled and minced

2 tablespoons olive oil

2 teaspoons chili powder

½ cup sliced black olives

1 (15-ounce) can enchilada sauce, divided

10 (8") whole-wheat flour tortillas

½ cup shredded vegan cheese

1. Preheat oven to 350°F.
2. In a large skillet over medium heat, cook tofu, mushrooms, onion, and garlic in oil for 5 minutes. Add in chili powder and mix up well, cooking for 1 minute more.
3. Remove from heat. Mix in olives and ⅔ cup enchilada sauce.
4. Lightly cover the bottom of an ungreased 9" × 13" casserole dish with ⅔ cup enchilada sauce.
5. Fill each tortilla with ¼ cup mushroom-tofu mixture, and roll up. Place in the casserole dish. Top with remaining enchilada sauce and cheese. Bake 30 minutes.

PART-TIME TIP

All breads, pizza doughs, and taco shells are typically vegan. However, it's always worth a glance at the ingredient list if you're unsure or using a new brand. Certain taco wraps are made with lard, and certain breads include buttermilk and egg.

Per Serving:
Calories: 895
Fat: 35 g
Protein: 29 g

Sodium: 2,696 mg
Fiber: 11 g
Carbohydrates: 115 g
Sugar: 18 g

SPICY SEITAN TACO "MEAT"

You can also make taco "meat" out of black beans or TVP. But seitan taco "meat" is better if you're looking for strip-shaped meat.

SERVES 6

½ medium yellow onion, peeled and diced

½ medium green bell pepper, seeded and chopped small

1 large tomato, chopped

1 (16-ounce) package prepared seitan, chopped (about 2½ cups)

2 tablespoons olive oil

1 tablespoon soy sauce

1 teaspoon hot sauce

2 tablespoons chili powder

½ teaspoon ground cumin

6 (8") white tortillas

1. In a large saucepan over medium-high heat, sauté onion, bell pepper, tomato, and seitan in oil for about 5 minutes until seitan is browned.

2. Add in soy sauce, hot sauce, chili powder, and cumin. Cook for 1 minute, and serve in tortillas!

Per Serving:
Calories: 273
Fat: 8 g
Protein: 18 g

Sodium: 848 mg
Fiber: 4 g
Carbohydrates: 32 g
Sugar: 5 g

BLACK BEAN AND BARLEY TACO SALAD

Craving the rich, tasty, meaty, mouthwatering satisfaction of Mexican food? Look no further. Barley adds a satisfying chewy fullness to this meal. *Su corazón ha sido capturado.* Translation: your heart has been captured.

SERVES 2

1 (15-ounce) can black beans, drained

½ teaspoon ground cumin

½ teaspoon dried oregano leaves

½ teaspoon onion powder

2 tablespoons lime juice

1 teaspoon hot chili sauce

1 cup cooked barley

1 medium head iceberg lettuce, shredded

1 cup crumbled blue corn tortilla chips

¾ cup organic salsa

2 tablespoons Dairy-Free Ranch Dressing (see recipe in Chapter 4)

1. In a medium bowl, mash up beans, cumin, oregano, onion powder, lime juice, and chili sauce. Add barley and mix well.
2. Layer two plates with alternating layers of lettuce, bean mixture, and chips, and top with salsa. Drizzle ranch dressing over tops, and serve.

Per Serving:
Calories: 457
Fat: 7 g
Protein: 19 g

Sodium: 1,154 mg
Fiber: 22 g
Carbohydrates: 83 g
Sugar: 10 g

CONFETTI "RICE"

Use in corn tortillas or on top of a salad for a Mexican twist. Any recipe with the word *confetti* in it has to be delicious and fun. Just don't throw it in the air. Or at least taste it first.

SERVES 6

1 medium yellow onion, peeled and chopped

2 cloves garlic, peeled and minced

2 tablespoons olive oil

1 cup barley

1 (15-ounce) can diced tomatoes, undrained

1 tablespoon soy sauce

2 cups vegetable broth

1 teaspoon ground cumin

1 teaspoon chili powder

½ teaspoon cayenne pepper

1 teaspoon onion powder

1 cup frozen corn, thawed

1 teaspoon chopped fresh Italian flat-leaf parsley

½ teaspoon salt

1. In a large stockpot over medium-high heat, sauté onion and garlic in oil 3 minutes. Add barley and stir, allowing to brown. Toast for 1 minute.
2. Add tomatoes plus juice, soy sauce, and broth. Stir well, and add cumin, chili powder, cayenne pepper, and onion powder. Cook for 15 minutes.
3. Add corn, parsley, and salt. Cook for another 5 minutes and serve.

Per Serving:
Calories: 219
Fat: 6 g
Protein: 6 g

Sodium: 730 mg
Fiber: 8 g
Carbohydrates: 39 g
Sugar: 5 g

BAKED MEXICAN TEMPEH

This sauce will make tempeh flavorful and perfect, whether you eat it alone or in tacos or low-cal lettuce wraps!

SERVES 4

1 cup vegetable broth

2 (8-ounce) packages tempeh, quartered

½ cup tomato paste

3 cloves garlic, peeled and minced

2 tablespoons soy sauce

2 tablespoons apple cider vinegar

3 tablespoons water

1½ teaspoons chili powder

½ teaspoon dried oregano leaves

¼ teaspoon cayenne pepper

⅛ teaspoon hot sauce

1. In a medium saucepan over medium-low heat, bring broth to a simmer (liquid should be moving, but no bubbles should be forming). Add tempeh and continue simmering for 10 minutes. Remove tempeh and drain.

2. In a small bowl, whisk together tomato paste, garlic, soy sauce, vinegar, water, chili powder, oregano, and cayenne pepper. Place tempeh in a shallow dish, and cover with marinade. Allow to marinate for at least 3 hours.

3. Preheat oven to 375°F.

4. Transfer tempeh into an ungreased 9" × 13" casserole dish, and baste slices well with marinade.

5. Bake for 17 minutes. Turn over, baste again, and cook for another 15 minutes. Top with hot sauce. *Ay, caramba.*

PART-TIME TIP

Tempeh can easily absorb sauces and marinades, but remember to simmer the tempeh chunks in water or veggie broth first in order to aid the process.

Per Serving:
Calories: 239
Fat: 13 g
Protein: 25 g

Sodium: 709 mg
Fiber: 1 g
Carbohydrates: 12 g
Sugar: 1 g

CHAPTER 9

SINFUL DESSERTS

COUNT YOUR VEGAN BLESSINGS

MAPLE DATE CARROT CAKE

A moist cake that would go great with a little vegan Vanilla Frosting (see recipe in this chapter). The pineapple juice in this recipe ties in subtly to the diced pineapple topping of Caramelized Onion and Barbecue Sauce Pizza (see recipe in Chapter 7), so why not serve them together?

SERVES 4

1½ cups raisins

1⅓ cups pineapple juice

6 dates, pitted and diced

2¼ cups grated carrot

½ cup maple syrup

¼ cup unsweetened applesauce

2 tablespoons olive oil

3 cups white whole-wheat flour

1½ teaspoons baking soda

½ teaspoon salt

1 teaspoon ground cinnamon

½ teaspoon ground allspice

Egg replacement mixture (equivalent of 2 eggs), prepared according to package directions

1. Preheat oven to 350°F. Grease a 9" cake pan with vegan margarine.
2. In a small bowl, mix raisins with pineapple juice, and let sit for 10 minutes. In another small bowl, soak dates in water for 10 minutes and then drain.
3. In a large bowl, mix raisins, pineapple juice, dates, carrot, syrup, applesauce, and oil.
4. In another large bowl, mix flour, baking soda, salt, cinnamon, and allspice. Mix wet ingredients into dry ingredients. Add egg replacement and mix.
5. Pour batter into the cake pan, and bake for 30 minutes. Make sure a toothpick comes out clean from the center of the cake before removing cake from the oven.

THE SKINNY ON...EGG REPLACER

If you're just looking to keep things moist when cooking, you need not use egg replacer. Try out applesauce, soy yogurt, jam, preserves, or even hummus!

Per Serving:
Calories: 770
Fat: 10 g
Protein: 11 g

Sodium: 484 mg
Fiber: 15 g
Carbohydrates: 174 g
Sugar: 101 g

COCOA-NUT-COCONUT NO-BAKE COOKIES

It wouldn't be an Italian Christmas without bite-sized macaroon cookies. This veganized version of the well-known favorite will have you grinning with delight, and perhaps even speaking some words *d'amore* to your neighbor. (So make sure you're sitting next to someone you like, or it could get pretty awkward.)

YIELDS 2 DOZEN COOKIES

¼ cup vegan margarine

¼ cup vanilla soy milk

2 cups granulated sugar

⅓ cup cocoa powder

½ cup almond butter

½ teaspoon vanilla extract

3 cups quick-cooking oats

½ cup finely chopped raw almonds

½ cup coconut flakes

1. Line a baking sheet with waxed paper.
2. In a large saucepan over low heat, heat margarine and milk for 1 minute until margarine has melted. Add sugar and cocoa. Stir and bring to a boil on high heat to dissolve sugar. Reduce heat back to low and add in almond butter, cooking 2 minutes until it's melted.
3. Remove from heat, and add in remaining ingredients.
4. Spoon out mixture in little balls onto waxed paper, and press them into a cookie shape. Chill until firm, about 2 hours.

Per Serving: 1 cookie
Calories: 182
Fat: 7 g
Protein: 4 g
Sodium: 34 mg
Fiber: 3 g
Carbohydrates: 27 g
Sugar: 18 g

COCONUT RICE PUDDING

Rice pudding is a traditional Mexican dessert. Try this jazzed-up vegan version as the perfect ending for your dinner menu. *Delicioso!* Your guests will be sure to say *gracias*.

SERVES 4

1½ cups vanilla soy milk

1½ cups sweetened coconut milk

1½ cups cooked white rice

2 tablespoons maple syrup

2 tablespoons agave nectar

5 dates, pitted and chopped

⅙ teaspoon ground cinnamon

2 medium mangos, peeled and chopped

1. In a large saucepan on low heat, mix soy milk, coconut milk, and rice together. Cook for 10 minutes until mixture thickens.
2. Add syrup, agave nectar, and dates. Cook for another 3 minutes.
3. Remove from heat, and let cool for about 5 minutes. Garnish with cinnamon and mangos.

Per Serving:
Calories: 383
Fat: 4 g
Protein: 6 g

Sodium: 57 mg
Fiber: 5 g
Carbohydrates: 86 g
Sugar: 61 g

CHOCOLATE CHIP COOKIES

The classic. But healthier, tastier, and all around better in every way.

YIELDS 2 DOZEN COOKIES

2/3 cup vegan margarine

2/3 cup granulated sugar

2/3 cup light brown sugar

1/3 cup unsweetened applesauce

1½ teaspoons vanilla extract

Egg replacement mixture (equivalent of 2 eggs), prepared according to package directions

2½ cups white whole-wheat flour

1 teaspoon baking soda

½ teaspoon baking powder

1 teaspoon salt

2/3 cup quick-cooking oats

1½ cups vegan chocolate chips

1. Preheat oven to 375°F.
2. Cream together margarine and granulated sugar in a large bowl. Add brown sugar, applesauce, vanilla, and egg replacer. Mix well.
3. In another large bowl, mix flour, baking soda, baking powder, and salt. Combine wet ingredients into dry ingredients. Mix well.
4. Stir in oats and chocolate chips until evenly dispersed throughout dough.
5. Use a spoon to drop little balls of dough onto a baking sheet very lightly greased with vegan margarine. Bake for 12 minutes.

Per Serving: 1 cookie
Calories: 186
Fat: 9 g
Protein: 2 g

Sodium: 213 mg
Fiber: 2 g
Carbohydrates: 28 g
Sugar: 18 g

GINGER SPICE COOKIES

It wouldn't be the holidays without a little ginger thrown in. It's an ingredient that seems to hearken back to all those memories of warm family get-togethers with laughter and cider and whiskey all aflow.

YIELDS 18 COOKIES

1/3 cup vegan margarine

1/2 cup maple syrup

1/3 cup molasses

1/4 cup plain sweetened almond milk

2 1/4 cups white whole-wheat flour

1 teaspoon baking powder

1/2 teaspoon baking soda

1/2 teaspoon ground cinnamon

1/2 teaspoon ground ginger

1/4 teaspoon ground allspice

1/2 teaspoon salt

1. Cream together margarine, syrup, molasses, and milk in a large bowl.
2. In another large bowl, mix flour, baking powder, baking soda, cinnamon, ginger, allspice, and salt.
3. Mix wet ingredients into dry ingredients. Chill covered in the refrigerator for 30 minutes.
4. Preheat oven to 350°F.
5. Roll up dough into 1 1/2" balls. Place balls on a baking sheet greased with vegan margarine, and pat them down a bit. Bake for 12 minutes. Keep an eye on them so the bottoms don't burn!

Per Serving: 1 cookie
Calories: 110
Fat: 4 g
Protein: 1 g

Sodium: 161 mg
Fiber: 1 g
Carbohydrates: 19 g
Sugar: 10 g

APRICOT GINGER SORBET

Cool, sweet, and healthy. Hardly any fat and complemented by chunks of fresh fruit.

SERVES 4

$^2/_3$ cup water

$^2/_3$ cup granulated sugar

2 teaspoons fresh minced ginger

5 cups chopped apricots

3 tablespoons lemon juice

1. In a large saucepan over medium heat, add water, sugar, and ginger. Bring to a boil, and then turn down heat to simmer on low. Cook for 4 minutes until sugar transforms into a syrup.
2. Purée cooked syrup with apricots and lemon juice in a food processor.
3. Pour mixture into a freezer-safe dish, and freeze covered for 4 hours. Stir every 30 minutes while freezing. It's a pain, but hey, sorbet is worth a little work, right?

Per Serving:
Calories: 235
Fat: 1 g
Protein: 3 g

Sodium: 3 mg
Fiber: 4 g
Carbohydrates: 58 g
Sugar: 53 g

TOFU CHOCOLATE PUDDING

The English do love their puddings, don't they? *Pudding* in the English sense can mean anything from a small moist cake to a custard to a rice pudding. It's a pretty loose term, so there is certainly space for a delicious you'll-never-guess-it-is-tofu dish.

SERVES 6

3 (1-pound) blocks silken tofu

¾ cup cocoa powder

1½ teaspoons vanilla extract

¾ cup all-natural peanut butter

¾ cup maple syrup

½ cup raisins, for garnish

Process all ingredients except raisins in a food processor until smooth and creamy. You may want to do this in two separate batches so you don't overload your food processor. Serve sprinkled with raisins.

Per Serving:
Calories: 486
Fat: 24 g
Protein: 21 g

Sodium: 25 mg
Fiber: 7 g
Carbohydrates: 58 g
Sugar: 38 g

FOOLPROOF VEGAN FUDGE

Rich and delicious, vegan fudge is just as good as the "real" stuff. So good, actually, that no one will ever know the difference. See, a little fraud may or may not be a good thing!

YIELDS 2 DOZEN 1" PIECES

1/2 cup vegan margarine

1/3 cup cocoa powder

1/3 cup soy cream

1/2 teaspoon vanilla extract

2 tablespoons all-natural peanut butter

3 1/2 cups powdered sugar

3/4 cup finely chopped walnuts

1. Grease an 8" × 8" square baking dish with vegan margarine.
2. In a medium saucepan on very low heat, melt margarine, cocoa, cream, vanilla, and peanut butter. Yum.
3. Add in powdered sugar little by little until mixture is thick. Add walnuts.
4. Quickly transfer mixture into the greased pan, and chill covered for 2 hours. Wait until completely firm to cut and serve. Voilà!

Per Serving: 1 (1") piece
Calories: 142
Fat: 7 g
Protein: 1 g

Sodium: 43 mg
Fiber: 1 g
Carbohydrates: 19 g
Sugar: 17 g

CHOCOLATE GRAHAM CRACKER CANDY BARS

Melty, gooey, delicious, and easy. Pretty much the recipe for SUCCESS, in capital letters.

YIELDS 16 BARS

1 cup almond butter

8 vegan graham crackers, quartered

1 cup vegan chocolate chips

$\frac{1}{4}$ cup vegan margarine

$\frac{1}{2}$ cup coconut flakes

$\frac{1}{4}$ cup chopped raw walnuts

1. Line a baking sheet with waxed paper.
2. Spread 1 tablespoon almond butter on each cracker, and top with another cracker to make a sandwich.
3. On very low heat, melt chocolate chips and margarine together in a small saucepan.
4. Using tongs, dip each cracker sandwich into melted chips to cover. Set the sandwiches back on the baking sheet, and sprinkle with coconut and walnuts.
5. Chill until firm, about 1 hour. Gobble up and send guests home with leftovers (or be greedy and keep them all to yourself!).

Per Serving: 1 bar
Calories: 211
Fat: 17 g
Protein: 4 g

Sodium: 83 mg
Fiber: 3 g
Carbohydrates: 13 g
Sugar: 8 g

STRAWBERRY MILKSHAKES

Who can resist a sweet strawberry treat before dinner? A direct throwback to childhood afternoons.

SERVES 6

1½ cups frozen whole strawberries

1½ (1-pound) blocks silken tofu

1 large banana, peeled

¾ cup apple juice

3 tablespoons maple syrup

12 ice cubes

6 scoops vanilla soy ice cream

Blend all ingredients except ice cream together in a blender. Pour into 6 tall glasses, and top each glass with 1 scoop ice cream.

Per Serving:
Calories: 232
Fat: 9 g
Protein: 7 g

Sodium: 71 mg
Fiber: 2 g
Carbohydrates: 31 g
Sugar: 22 g

EASY BANANA DATE COOKIES

Chewy, soft, and packed with sweet sugary goodness, dates pair well with soooo many dishes. A cookie similar to this is eaten in the Muslim communities of North Africa. Just a little fact for you.

YIELDS 1 DOZEN COOKIES

1 cup pitted, chopped dates

1 medium banana, peeled

1/2 teaspoon vanilla extract

1 3/4 cups coconut flakes

1/4 cup chopped raw almonds

1. Preheat oven to 375°F. Soak dates in water for 10 minutes in a small bowl, then drain.
2. Process dates, banana, and vanilla in a food processor. Get it smooth! Stir in coconut and almonds by hand until batter is thick.
3. Drop small globs of batter onto a baking sheet lightly greased with vegan margarine, and cook for 12 minutes. Eat them warm.

Per Serving: 1 cookie
Calories: 152
Fat: 10 g
Protein: 2 g

Sodium: 5 mg
Fiber: 4 g
Carbohydrates: 15 g
Sugar: 10 g

FROM-SCRATCH CHOCOLATE CAKE WITH VANILLA FROSTING

Um, hold the phone. Heavy, dense, and delicious, this vegan chocolate cake is just as good, if not better, than "normal" chocolate cake.

SERVES 6

FROM-SCRATCH CHOCOLATE CAKE

1½ cups whole-wheat flour

¾ cup granulated sugar

⅓ cup dark cocoa powder

1 teaspoon baking soda

1 cup sweetened soy milk

¼ cup unsweetened applesauce

2 tablespoons olive oil

1 tablespoon rice vinegar

1 teaspoon vanilla extract

VANILLA FROSTING

¼ cup vanilla soy milk

⅓ cup vegan margarine

2 teaspoons vanilla extract

3½ cups powdered sugar

1. **TO MAKE FROM-SCRATCH CHOCOLATE CAKE:** Preheat oven to 350°F. Grease a round 9" cake pan with vegan margarine.
2. Mix flour, sugar, cocoa, and baking soda in a large bowl.
3. In a medium bowl, mix milk, applesauce, oil, vinegar, and vanilla.
4. Combine wet and dry mixtures. Pour into the pan, and cook for about 28 minutes. Test the center with a toothpick. If it comes out clean, you're all set.
5. Let cool 20 minutes.
6. **TO MAKE VANILLA FROSTING:** Combine all ingredients in a food processor, adding powdered sugar last. Drizzle over cake.

Per Serving:
Calories: 643
Fat: 16 g
Protein: 6 g

Sodium: 340 mg
Fiber: 5 g
Carbohydrates: 123 g
Sugar: 97 g

STRAWBERRY COCONUT ICE CREAM

Luscious, rich, and everything that ice cream should be. Oh, except the bad-for-you part.

SERVES 6

2 cups coconut cream

1³/₄ cups frozen whole strawberries

³/₄ cup granulated sugar

2 teaspoons vanilla extract

¹/₄ teaspoon salt

1. Purée all ingredients in a food processor until smooth.
2. Pour into a large freezer-safe dish, and freeze 4 hours. Stir every 30 minutes while freezing.

PART-TIME TIP

If the ice cream gets too hard to stir, place it in the food processor again. Blend, and then return it to the freezer and continue stirring every 30 minutes.

Per Serving:
Calories: 479
Fat: 17 g
Protein: 1 g

Sodium: 135 mg
Fiber: 1 g
Carbohydrates: 83 g
Sugar: 79 g

PUMPKIN MAPLE PIE

Perfect with a little vanilla soy ice cream. This healthier version of a holiday classic will definitely give you bragging rights at Thanksgiving.

SERVES 8

1 (16-ounce) can pumpkin purée

½ cup maple syrup

1 (12-ounce) block silken tofu

¼ cup granulated sugar

1½ teaspoons ground cinnamon

½ teaspoon ground ginger

½ teaspoon ground nutmeg

¼ teaspoon ground cloves

½ teaspoon salt

1 Vegan Cookie Pie Crust (see recipe in this chapter)

1. Preheat oven to 400°F.
2. Simply combine all ingredients except pie crust until well mixed. Press Vegan Cookie Pie Crust into a greased 9" pie plate. Pour mixture into pie crust. Bake for 1 hour.
3. Cool for 30 minutes before serving. The pie will set as it cools.

Per Serving:
Calories: 515
Fat: 18 g
Protein: 6 g

Sodium: 715 mg
Fiber: 6 g
Carbohydrates: 86 g
Sugar: 53 g

VEGAN COOKIE PIE CRUST

The perfect all-vegan, all-delicious pie crust for any dessert you ever encounter.

SERVES 8

25 small vegan cookies (try any cookie recipe from this chapter!)

¼ cup melted vegan margarine

½ teaspoon vanilla extract

1. Process cookies in a food processor until ground up.
2. Add margarine and vanilla slowly, and blend.
3. Press mixture into a greased 9" pie plate, and pour desired filling on top before baking.

Per Serving:
Calories: 393
Fat: 17 g
Protein: 4 g

Sodium: 562 mg
Fiber: 4 g
Carbohydrates: 60 g
Sugar: 33 g

CHOCOLATE MOCHA FROSTING

You can never have too many frosting recipes. If you're feeling frisky, pair this with the From-Scratch Chocolate Cake (see recipe in this chapter) for something truly decadent.

SERVES 8

¼ cup strong black coffee, cooled

⅓ cup vegan margarine

2 teaspoons vanilla extract

⅓ cup cocoa powder

3 cups powdered sugar

1. Mix coffee, margarine, and vanilla together in a medium bowl. Make sure it's smooth and uniform. Add cocoa.
2. Slowly add in powdered sugar. Consistency should be rich and smooth.

Per Serving:
Calories: 253
Fat: 8 g
Protein: 1 g

Sodium: 82 mg
Fiber: 1 g
Carbohydrates: 47 g
Sugar: 44 g

CHOCOLATE MOCHA ICE CREAM

Have a coffee lover (or five) in the family? Woo them with this: vegan ice cream and coffee combined, vegan style. They won't be able to deny you. It's like a magic spell, but it tastes better.

SERVES 6

1 cup vegan chocolate chips

1 cup plain sweetened almond milk

1 (12-ounce) block silken tofu

1/3 cup granulated sugar

2 tablespoons instant coffee

2 teaspoons vanilla extract

1/4 teaspoon salt

1. In a small saucepan over very low heat, melt chocolate chips until smooth. Stir often so it doesn't burn in the pan.
2. In a blender, blend milk, tofu, sugar, coffee, vanilla, and salt. Keep blending until you get a creamy consistency. This might take 4 minutes, depending on your blender. Add melted chips and blend until smooth.
3. Pour mixture into a large freezer-proof dish. Place covered in the freezer for 4 hours. Stir every 30 minutes while freezing.

Per Serving:
Calories: 232
Fat: 10 g
Protein: 4 g

Sodium: 129 mg
Fiber: 2 g
Carbohydrates: 34 g
Sugar: 30 g

RASPBERRY LEMON CUPCAKES

Give these to a sweetheart on Valentine's Day. Or hog them all to yourself if you don't have a valentine.

YIELDS 18 CUPCAKES

- ½ cup vegan margarine, softened
- 1 cup granulated sugar
- ½ teaspoon vanilla extract
- ¾ cup vanilla soy milk
- ½ teaspoon lemon extract
- 2 tablespoons lemon juice
- Zest from 2 lemons
- 1¾ cups white whole-wheat flour
- 1½ teaspoons baking powder
- ½ teaspoon baking soda
- ¼ teaspoon salt
- ¾ cup diced fresh raspberries

1. Preheat oven to 350°F. Grease muffin tins with vegan margarine.
2. Beat margarine and sugar together in a large bowl. Add vanilla, milk, lemon extract, lemon juice, and lemon zest, and beat until blended.
3. In a different large bowl, sift together flour, baking powder, baking soda, and salt. Mix wet ingredients into dry ingredients. Carefully fold in raspberries.
4. Pour batter so each muffin cup is ¾ full. Bake for 17 minutes. Lovely!

Per Serving: 1 cupcake
Calories: 126
Fat: 5 g
Protein: 1 g
Sodium: 155 mg
Fiber: 1 g
Carbohydrates: 19 g
Sugar: 12 g

CHOCOLATE PEANUT BUTTER EXPLOSION PIE

It may not be healthy, but it is delicious. It also has the word *explosion* in the title. Honestly, who cares about a little excess every once in a while? Chocolate and peanut butter are like the Romeo and Juliet of the food world. And after all, isn't it time you were a little more romantic?

SERVES 8

¾ cup vegan chocolate chips

1 (12-ounce) block silken tofu

1¼ cups all-natural peanut butter, divided

½ cup plus 2 tablespoons vanilla soy milk, divided

1 Vegan Cookie Pie Crust (see recipe in this chapter)

2½ cups powdered sugar

2 tablespoons rice whipped cream

1. Melt chocolate chips in a small saucepan over very low heat.
2. Purée tofu, ½ cup peanut butter, and 2 tablespoons milk in a food processor. Add melted chocolate chips. Continue blending until everything is smooth.
3. Press Vegan Cookie Pie Crust into a greased 9" pie plate. Pour mixture into pie crust and chill for 1 hour.
4. In a medium saucepan on low heat, melt ¾ cup peanut butter, ½ cup milk, and powdered sugar. Spread mixture over cooled pie, and return to the refrigerator to chill for 30 minutes until firm. Serve topped with rice whipped cream.

Per Serving:
Calories: 889
Fat: 44 g
Protein: 16 g

Sodium: 585 mg
Fiber: 8 g
Carbohydrates: 119 g
Sugar: 83 g

CHEWY OATMEAL RAISIN COOKIES

Who on this earth doesn't like oatmeal raisin cookies? Eat them with a tall glass of almond milk. Leave them out for old St. Nick, or keep them all to yourself. (He gets enough cookies, come to think of it.)

YIELDS 18 COOKIES

- 1/3 cup vegan margarine, softened
- 1/2 cup light brown sugar
- 1/4 cup granulated sugar
- 1/3 cup unsweetened applesauce
- 1 teaspoon vanilla extract
- 2 tablespoons vanilla soy milk
- 3/4 cup whole-wheat flour
- 1/2 teaspoon baking soda
- 1/2 teaspoon ground cinnamon
- 1/2 teaspoon ground ginger
- 1 3/4 cups quick-cooking oats
- 2/3 cup raisins

1. Preheat oven to 350°F.
2. Mix margarine and sugars in a large bowl until smooth. Add applesauce, vanilla, and milk. Combine well.
3. Sift flour, baking soda, cinnamon, and ginger together in a large bowl. Mix wet ingredients into dry ingredients. Stir in the oats and raisins last.
4. Drop round balls of dough onto a baking sheet greased with vegan margarine, and bake for 12 minutes.

Per Serving: 1 cookie
Calories: 138
Fat: 4 g
Protein: 2 g
Sodium: 75 mg
Fiber: 2 g
Carbohydrates: 23 g
Sugar: 13 g

VERY BERRY BANANA COOKIES

A sweet and unfamiliar treat. The combination of blueberry preserves, dried blueberries, cranberries, and the pinch of cinnamon will have you smacking your lips and coming back for seconds—and thirds.

YIELDS 1 DOZEN COOKIES

1¾ cups whole-wheat flour

1 teaspoon baking powder

¼ teaspoon salt

¼ teaspoon ground cinnamon

½ cup blueberry preserves

½ cup plain sweetened almond milk

¾ cup rolled oats

1 medium banana, peeled

½ cup dried cranberries

¼ cup dried blueberries

12 raw almonds

1. Preheat oven to 350°F.
2. Combine flour, baking powder, salt, cinnamon, preserves, and milk in a large bowl. Mix well.
3. Mix in oats. Add banana into batter by mashing with a fork. Fold in dried cranberries and blueberries.
4. Roll dough into 1½" balls, and place on a baking sheet well-greased with vegan margarine. Press an almond into the center of each little cookie. Cook for about 22 minutes. Keep checking to make certain the bottoms don't burn and the middles aren't mushy!

Per Serving: 1 cookie
Calories: 136
Fat: 1 g
Protein: 2 g
Sodium: 90 mg
Fiber: 3 g
Carbohydrates: 30 g
Sugar: 16 g

EASY BLACKBERRY CORN BREAD

This corn bread is perfect if you don't enjoy the overly saccharine heaviness of some corn bread recipes. The sweetness comes entirely from the fresh, ripe blackberries. The dark juice bleeds into the corn, and is Just. Plain. Delicious.

YIELDS 1 DOZEN PIECES

1³/₄ cups cornmeal

1 teaspoon baking powder

¹/₂ cup plain sweetened almond milk

1 (6-ounce) container vanilla soy yogurt

1 (8-ounce) bag frozen corn, thawed

1 teaspoon honey

2 pints fresh blackberries, divided

1. Preheat oven to 350°F.
2. Mix cornmeal, baking powder, milk, and yogurt together in a large bowl until everything sticks together.
3. Fold in corn and honey. Gently fold 1¹/₂ pints blackberries, taking care not to break them.
4. Press mixture into a 9" × 13" baking dish greased with vegan margarine, and press remaining blackberries into the top of batter. Cook for about 30 minutes.

Per Serving: 1 piece
Calories: 120
Fat: 1 g
Protein: 3 g

Sodium: 45 mg
Fiber: 6 g
Carbohydrates: 25 g
Sugar: 5 g

PERFECT PUMPKIN BREAD

This pumpkin bread is fast, simple, and infused with the homey flavors of autumn. Eat it with jam for breakfast, vegan margarine as a snack or side, or underneath some soy vanilla ice cream for dessert!

YIELDS 1 DOZEN PIECES

1¾ cups whole-wheat flour

⅔ cup puréed pumpkin

1 (6-ounce) container vanilla soy yogurt

½ cup plus ¼ cup quick-cooking oats, divided

¼ cup plain sweetened almond milk

1 teaspoon honey

¾ teaspoon ground cinnamon

½ teaspoon ground nutmeg

¼ cup raw walnuts

1. Preheat oven to 400°F.
2. In a large bowl, combine flour with pumpkin, yogurt, and ½ cup oats. Mix well to form a dough.
3. Add milk and continue mixing. Fold in honey, cinnamon, and nutmeg.
4. Grease a 9" × 13" baking pan with vegan margarine. Roll dough into a loaf shape. Top with remaining ¼ cup oats and walnuts. Cook for 40 minutes, checking the bottom of bread to make sure it's browned but not burned!

Per Serving: 2 pieces
Calories: 239
Fat: 6 g
Protein: 8 g

Sodium: 12 mg
Fiber: 7 g
Carbohydrates: 41 g
Sugar: 6 g

VEGAN CHOCOLATE COCONUT ICE CREAM

Almost all non-vegan recipes can be turned vegan by simply substituting the non-vegan fat (usually milk or butter) with a vegan fat (nuts). This frequently yields absolutely incredible results that are—dare we say—better than the originals.

YIELDS 1½ PINTS

1 cup raw cashews

1 cup pecans

1¾ cups water

2½ teaspoons vanilla extract

1 cup maple syrup

¼ cup dark cocoa powder

¼ teaspoon instant coffee

1 cup coconut flakes

1. Put all ingredients except coconut into a food processor and blend until smooth. Add coconut and pulse 3 times.
2. If you don't have an ice cream maker, just pop this puppy into a plastic container, cover, and stick in the freezer overnight.

Per Serving: ⅔ cup
Calories: 303
Fat: 20 g
Protein: 5 g

Sodium: 11 mg
Fiber: 4 g
Carbohydrates: 31 g
Sugar: 22 g

QUINOA "TAPIOCA" PUDDING

An untraditional dessert pudding, using healthy quinoa rather than rice. Delicious and creamy, this dish pairs nicely with a hot vegan cappuccino.

SERVES 4

1 cup quinoa

2 cups water

2 cups soy cream

2 tablespoons maple syrup

1 teaspoon cornstarch

2 large bananas, peeled and sliced

1/2 teaspoon almond extract

1/3 cup raisins

1/6 teaspoon ground nutmeg

1. In a large stockpot over high heat, add quinoa and water and bring to a boil. Reduce heat to low and simmer, covered, for 15 minutes. Mixture will be done when water is completely absorbed.
2. Add cream, syrup, cornstarch, and bananas to pot. Stir frequently, cooking for another 8 minutes.
3. Remove from heat. Stir in almond extract and raisins, and sprinkle with nutmeg.

Per Serving:
Calories: 491
Fat: 23 g
Protein: 10 g

Sodium: 71 mg
Fiber: 6 g
Carbohydrates: 63 g
Sugar: 25 g

DEATH BY RAW CHOCOLATE VEGAN "CHEESE" CAKE

Are you looking for the perfect dish to convince your skeptical friends that you haven't completely gone off the deep end with this vegan malarkey? You have come to the right place! When we say "cheese" cake, we do truly mean that this tastes like cheese-cake. This dish is going to knock your *Kinda Vegan*–doubting friends out.

SERVES 12

CRUST

½ cup pecans

½ cup raw walnuts

2 tablespoons cacao nibs

3 tablespoons agave nectar

⅙ teaspoon salt

FILLING

½ cup coconut oil

3½ cups raw cashews, soaked for 4 hours

4 dates, pitted

¾ cup agave nectar

½ cup maple syrup

½ teaspoon instant coffee

½ cup water

2 teaspoons vanilla extract

½ cup cocoa powder

½ cup dark cocoa powder

⅙ teaspoon salt

1 (5-ounce) bag pretzels, crushed

1. **TO MAKE CRUST:** Blend all ingredients in a food processor. Crust should have a "choppy" look to it, so don't blend too much.

2. Press crust mixture into a greased 9" pie plate, covering the entire surface area.

3. **TO MAKE FILLING:** Melt coconut oil by placing it into a plastic bag and setting the sealed bag in a small bowl of hot water.

4. Combine all ingredients except pretzels in a food processor and blend for 3 minutes. The texture should be creamy, the taste dense and rich.

5. Spoon filling mixture out onto crust. Then top with crumbled pretzels, and stick in the freezer for 2 hours to let the cheesecake "set." It will *not* freeze; don't worry.

6. Allow to defrost in the refrigerator for 30 minutes before serving. After defrosting, the "cheese" cake may be stored, covered with aluminum foil, in the refrigerator for up to 1 week.

Per Serving:
Calories: 570
Fat: 35 g
Protein: 10 g

Sodium: 221 mg
Fiber: 6 g
Carbohydrates: 63 g
Sugar: 36 g

265

LEMON POPPY CHEWY CAKE WITH BLUEBERRY DRIZZLE

This colorful, fragrant recipe will make lemon lovers go gaga. It's a great summertime cake that has a unique dense texture. Decorate the top with whole blueberries to really impress your friends.

SERVES 12

LEMON POPPY CHEWY CAKE

3 cups whole-wheat flour

1 teaspoon baking soda

1 teaspoon baking powder

1/2 teaspoon salt

3 1/2 teaspoons poppy seeds

2 teaspoons vanilla extract

1/3 cup lemon juice

1 cup apple juice

2/3 cup maple syrup

Zest of 3 lemons

1 pint fresh blueberries

BLUEBERRY DRIZZLE

1/2 cup fresh blueberries

1/2 cup vegan margarine

3 cups powdered sugar

1 tablespoon lemon juice

1/2 teaspoon strawberry extract

1/2 teaspoon apple cider vinegar

1. **TO MAKE LEMON POPPY CHEWY CAKE:** Preheat oven to 350°F.
2. Mix flour, baking soda, baking powder, salt, and poppy seeds together in a large bowl. Add vanilla, lemon juice, apple juice, and syrup. Add lemon zest.
3. Grease a 9" pie plate with vegan margarine. Fill with batter. Bake 35 minutes.
4. **TO MAKE BLUEBERRY DRIZZLE:** Simply combine all ingredients in a food processor, and drizzle on top of cooled cake.

PART-TIME TIP

Aside from adding apple cider vinegar to a lot of vegan recipes to curd almond or soy milk, you can use to it give a kick to recipes that usually call for cheese. Adding it to this drizzle creates an almost "cream cheesy" flavor!

Per Serving:
Calories: 368
Fat: 9 g
Protein: 4 g

Sodium: 317 mg
Fiber: 4 g
Carbohydrates: 71 g
Sugar: 46 g

RAW TO DIE FOR APPLE PIE WITH BERRY TOPPING

This apple pie is free of butter and refined sugar, and you'll love yourself for eating it. No more regret after dessert! A word of warning: this pie is best made and eaten on the same day; otherwise, the natural juices of the apples will make the crust soggy!

SERVES 12

CRUST

½ cup dried cranberries

2 cups pecans

½ cup raw walnuts

½ cup pitted dates

FILLING

6 medium Gala apples, peeled and cored

2 teaspoons honey

2 teaspoons ground cinnamon

½ cup raisins

½ cup rolled oats

¾ cup pitted dates

BERRY TOPPING

¾ cup dried cranberries

2 tablespoons honey

1 cup fresh red grapes

¾ cup water

1 cup fresh blueberries

1. **TO MAKE CRUST:** Process all ingredients in a food processor. Press mixture into the bottom of a greased 9" pie plate.

2. **TO MAKE FILLING:** Add ½ of apples to a food processor and process. If you add more than this at a time, you may overwhelm the machine.

3. Add honey, cinnamon, and raisins to apple mixture, and process together. Place mixture in a medium bowl.

4. Process remaining apples, then add back first apple mixture and process both apple mixtures together. Add oats and dates, and process for another 2 minutes.

5. Spoon apple mixture into crust. Set in the freezer for 1 hour.

6. **TO MAKE BERRY TOPPING:** Process all ingredients together in a food processor. Set aside in the refrigerator until serving time. Dollop on top of pie when ready to serve. Yummmm!

Per Serving:
Calories: 366
Fat: 17 g
Protein: 4 g

Sodium: 4 mg
Fiber: 8 g
Carbohydrates: 58 g
Sugar: 43 g

APPENDIX: MEAL PLANS

THE SOPHISTICATED SWEET TOOTH

Serves 4

APPETIZER: Spicy Sweet Cucumber Salad (Chapter 4)

MAIN COURSE: Caramelized Onion and Barbecue Sauce Pizza (Chapter 7)

DESSERT: Maple Date Carrot Cake (Chapter 9)

THE MAMMA MIA

Serves 4

APPETIZER: White Bean and Orzo Minestrone (Chapter 5)

MAIN COURSE: Breaded Eggplant "Parmesan" (Chapter 8)

DESSERT: Cocoa-Nut-Coconut No-Bake Cookies (Chapter 9)

THE AY CARAMBA

Serves 4

APPETIZER: Nacho "Cheese" Dip (Chapter 3)

MAIN COURSE: Tofu and Portobello "Enchiladas" (Chapter 8)

DESSERT: Coconut Rice Pudding (Chapter 9)

THE WAY EASIER THAN IT SHOULD BE

Serves 4

APPETIZER: Vegan "Pigs" in a Blanket (Chapter 3)

MAIN COURSE: So Incredibly Easy Black Bean Burgers (Chapter 7)

DESSERT: Chocolate Chip Cookies (Chapter 9)

THE ANYTIME THANKSGIVING
Serves 4
APPETIZER: Cashew Cream of Asparagus Soup (Chapter 5)
MAIN COURSE: Sweet Stuffed Butternut Squash (Chapter 6)
DESSERT: Ginger Spice Cookies (Chapter 9)

THE ZEN MOMENT
Serves 4
APPETIZER: Udon Noodle Buddha Bowl (Chapter 8)
MAIN COURSE: Sesame Baked Tofu (Chapter 8)
DESSERT: Apricot Ginger Sorbet (Chapter 9)

THE QUITE RIGHT AND PROPER DINNER
Serves 6
APPETIZER: Vegan Cheese Ball (Chapter 3)
MAIN COURSE: No Shepherd, No Sheep Pie (Chapter 7)
DESSERT: Tofu Chocolate Pudding (Chapter 9)

THE BACKYARD BBQ WANNABE
Serves 6
APPETIZER: Tempeh Dill "Chicken" Salad (Chapter 7)
MAIN COURSE: Seitan Barbecue "Meat" (Chapter 7)
DESSERT: Chocolate Graham Cracker Candy Bars (Chapter 9)

THE HOW IS THIS NOT A MILLION CALORIES?

Serves 4

APPETIZER: Classic Green Bean Casserole (Chapter 6)

MAIN COURSE: TVP, Mushroom, and White Wine Stroganoff (Chapter 7)

DESSERT: Foolproof Vegan Fudge (Chapter 9)

THE COMFORT FOOD FEAST (OR, "LIKE HOW MOM USED TO MAKE")

Serves 6

APPETIZER: Strawberry Milkshakes (Chapter 9)

MAIN COURSE: Super-Meaty TVP Meatloaf (Chapter 7)

DESSERT: From-Scratch Chocolate Cake with Vanilla Frosting (Chapter 9)

THE EASYGOING MEDITERRANEAN

Serves 4

APPETIZER: Eggplant Baba Ghanoush (Chapter 3)

MAIN COURSE: Easy Falafel Patties (Chapter 6)

DESSERT: Easy Banana Date Cookies (Chapter 9)

US/METRIC CONVERSION CHART

VOLUME CONVERSIONS

US VOLUME MEASURE	METRIC EQUIVALENT
⅛ teaspoon	0.5 milliliter
¼ teaspoon	1 milliliter
½ teaspoon	2 milliliters
1 teaspoon	5 milliliters
½ tablespoon	7 milliliters
1 tablespoon (3 teaspoons)	15 milliliters
2 tablespoons (1 fluid ounce)	30 milliliters
¼ cup (4 tablespoons)	60 milliliters
⅓ cup	80 milliliters
½ cup (4 fluid ounces)	125 milliliters
⅔ cup	160 milliliters
¾ cup (6 fluid ounces)	180 milliliters
1 cup (16 tablespoons)	250 milliliters
1 pint (2 cups)	500 milliliters
1 quart (4 cups)	1 liter (about)

WEIGHT CONVERSIONS

US WEIGHT MEASURE	METRIC EQUIVALENT
½ ounce	15 grams
1 ounce	30 grams
2 ounces	60 grams
3 ounces	85 grams
¼ pound (4 ounces)	115 grams
½ pound (8 ounces)	225 grams
¾ pound (12 ounces)	340 grams
1 pound (16 ounces)	454 grams

OVEN TEMPERATURE CONVERSIONS

DEGREES FAHRENHEIT	DEGREES CELSIUS
200 degrees F	95 degrees C
250 degrees F	120 degrees C
275 degrees F	135 degrees C
300 degrees F	150 degrees C
325 degrees F	160 degrees C
350 degrees F	180 degrees C
375 degrees F	190 degrees C
400 degrees F	205 degrees C
425 degrees F	220 degrees C
450 degrees F	230 degrees C

BAKING PAN SIZES

AMERICAN	METRIC
8 × 1½ inch round baking pan	20 × 4 cm cake tin
9 × 1½ inch round baking pan	23 × 3.5 cm cake tin
11 × 7 × 1½ inch baking pan	28 × 18 × 4 cm baking tin
13 × 9 × 2 inch baking pan	30 × 20 × 5 cm baking tin
2 quart rectangular baking dish	30 × 20 × 3 cm baking tin
15 × 10 × 2 inch baking pan	38 × 25 × 5 cm baking tin (Swiss roll tin)
9 inch pie plate	22 × 4 or 23 × 4 cm pie plate
7 or 8 inch springform pan	18 or 20 cm springform or loose bottom cake tin
9 × 5 × 3 inch loaf pan	23 × 13 × 7 cm or 2 lb narrow loaf or pâté tin
1½ quart casserole	1.5 liter casserole
2 quart casserole	2 liter casserole

INDEX